EXPANDED EDITION

The Intimate Mystery

CREATING STRENGTH AND

BEAUTY IN YOUR MARRIAGE

DAN ALLENDER
and TREMPER LONGMAN III

IVP Books

An imprint of InterVarsity Press
Downers Grove, Illinois

InterVarsity Press
P.O. Box 1400, Downers Grove, IL 60515-1426
World Wide Web: www.ivpress.com
E-mail: email@ivpress.com

Expanded edition ©2009 by Dan Allender and Tremper Longman III
First edition ©2005 by Dan Allender and Tremper Longman III

InterVarsity Press® is the book-publishing division of InterVarsity Christian Fellowship/USA®, a movement of students and faculty active on campus at hundreds of universities, colleges and schools of nursing in the United States of America, and a member movement of the International Fellowship of Evangelical Students. For information about local and regional activities, write Public Relations Dept., InterVarsity Christian Fellowship/USA, 6400 Schroeder Rd.,P.O. Box 7895, Madison, WI 53707-7895, or visit the IVCF website at <www.intervarsity.org>.

Unless otherwise indicated, all Scripture quotations are taken from the Holy Bible, New Living Translation, copyright ©1996, 2004. Used by permission Tyndale House Publishers, Inc., Wheaton, Illinois 60189. All rights reserved.

Design: Cindy Kiple
Images: Gandee Vasan/Getty Images

ISBN 978-0-8308-3724-8

Printed in the United States of America ∞

Library of Congress Cataloging-in-Publication Data

Allender, Dan B.
    The intimate mystery: creating strength and beauty in your marriage
    /Dan Allender and Tremper Longman III.
       p.cm.—(Intimate marriage series)
    ISBN 0-8308-2131-7 (alk. paper)
    1. Marriage—Religious aspects—Christianity. I. Longman, Tremper.
    II. Title. III. Series.
    BV835.A4556 2005
    248.8'44—dc22
                                                                    2005004494

P   18   17   16   15   14   13   12   11   10   9   8   7   6   5   4   3   2   1
Y   24   23   22   21   20   19   18   17   16   15   14   13   12   11   10   09

To Alice and Rebecca

Her children rise up and bless her;
   her husband praises her:
"Many women act nobly,
   but you surpass all of them!" (Proverbs 31:28-29)

Contents

1 A MAN'S BEST FRIEND . . . IS NOT A DOG 9

2 THE MEANING OF MARRIAGE 17

3 THE MATRIX OF MARRIAGE 27

4 LEAVING: *Making Space for Faithfulness* 35

5 LEAVING: *Walking Away from Home* 45

6 WEAVING: *Connecting Communication* 57

7 WEAVING: *Bringing Our Souls Together* 67

8 CLEAVING: *United into One Flesh* 77

9 CLEAVING: *Playing with Glory* 89

10 IN THE GARDEN 99

BONUS SECTION: THE GOAL OF MARRIAGE STUDY

Welcome to Intimate Marriage Bible Studies 107

1 Knowing Who We Are as Husband and Wife
  Genesis 1:26-31; 2:7 111

2 Leaving—from the Male Perspective
  Genesis 2 117

3 Leaving—from the Female Perspective
   Psalm 45:10-15 123

4 Weaving
   Ecclesiastes 4:7-12 127

5 Cleaving
   Genesis 2:18-25 132

6 The Ultimate Loyalty
   Psalm 127 136

ONE

A Man's Best Friend . . . Is Not a Dog

It shouldn't have been so hard. It certainly ought not to have taken so long or cost so much money. It was just one small, six-pound ball of fur. Without any cognizance of what this being would bring to our family, we chose to buy a dog.

Maggie is the family beast. She is an Australian terrier or, as we more often refer to her, a Down-Under Terror. She has become a symbol of all that is difficult, silly, stupid, crazy and good about our family and marriage. Her story is our story.

Maggie came after we had given away our second dog, a wild and unruly Dalmatian. She was given to friends when we discovered that she liked to stand over our second child, Amanda, remove her boots and gloves and keep her pinned to the snow.

Maggie's presence came through a brief, irrational moment of fear on my part that our children would hate us if they didn't grow up with a pet. In fact, Maggie has been the source of much travail and terror in our family life.

She was only eight weeks old when she fell out of Amanda's hands two flights to a concrete floor during an early-morning snowstorm. She was rushed unconscious and limp to a neighbor who was a veterinarian.

She lived, but ever since that accident I have been convinced that she suffered brain damage.

I didn't help her condition when I ran over her with my car the day we were to move from Colorado to Washington State. She bounced along the pavement against the underbelly of the carriage of the car for thirty yards. The remainder of the day she refused to get near any Allender, so she was put into the moving van by a kind neighbor.

In another odd act of terror, she got into a dogfight with a ninety-pound German shepherd and was torn in two, requiring 250 stitches. She was saved from death by my wife's heroic and foolish decision to jump into the middle of the fight and pluck Maggie from the shepherd's jaws.

All said, she is a feisty, unruly, conniving, odd beast of a pet. But she is ours, we love her, and we pay vet bills rather than put her to sleep. We complain and nag her, but more often than not on a cold winter morning one of us will pick her up, take her downstairs and snuggle with her in front of the fire. I could shoot her, but we would suffer great harm to protect her.

Is it far-fetched or sacrilegious to say I feel the same—and my wife feels the same—about our marriage? It has had accidents. At times it seems brain-damaged, at least crazy. We have run over each other and been chewed by predators in our neighborhood, church, work and friendships. We have both risked imminent harm to jump into a melee to save what we love. And we have both had surgeries, have been sewn back together more times than we can count, and have the scars to prove it.

There are days I'd like to pack off my wife with a one-way ticket to a faraway land. And then I come to my senses, no matter the problem or hurt, and realize that she is the finest, greatest gift God has given me and will ever give me in this life.

After twenty-seven years we are a ragtag, unruly, feisty, odd couple; we love each other more than when we were married and our God more than when we were first confessed him as our Master. Nonetheless, marriage is a muddle.

THE MUDDLE OF MARRIAGE

There are three huge potholes that muddle up the process of marriage: past baggage, contempt for differences and failure to grow. Each muddle overlaps and spills into the other two, but they are distinctive enough to bear some reflection.

Past baggage. We are fully fouled up before we ever meet our spouse. And we wander into marriage with our bags packed full of clothes that are a long way from being clean. Nonetheless, we hide it well. In fact, there is likely no period of greater deception in any relationship than courtship.

I knew my Becky was a hiker and outdoorswoman, a lover of the wild. I affected the same interests, bought hiking shoes and promised we would hike the Appalachian Trail during our first year of marriage. I can't recall whether I was sincere and deluded by love, lust and hope or whether I was lying out of my brain and figured that once we were married I would have to fess up. All I know is I am not fond of hiking, the out-of-doors scares me, and we've been married nearly three decades but have not walked, hiked, skipped or jumped the Appalachian Trail.

If that had been the only conscious or unwitting deception, we would have suffered, but very little. In fact, I didn't tell her about my past sexual abuse. Nor did I mention that my parents were fond of only the girls I broke up with. I didn't share much about my eruptions of anger or how absorbed I could become in a book. I didn't share a thing about what past girlfriends had said to me in the heat and heartache of a breakup. I was quite silent on my deficiencies, past influences and neurotic tendencies. I figured if she didn't notice it, maybe it didn't exist.

Something magical happens after the honeymoon—for some couples it happens smack dab in the middle: the past finds its way back to its rightful owner. Unfortunately, the past debts are now the responsibility of the new spouse. And in some cases these unbidden intruders never leave, never get addressed, and sap the energy and life out of the marriage.

This muddle is addressed by God when he tells a young married couple to leave their mother and father. We can't hope to deal with the past until it is named, and once it is owned up to, we are to break all loyalty to anything that once owned, ruled or controlled us. Otherwise the pothole will one day become a grand canyon between husband and wife.

Contempt for differences. I loved my wife's quiet and gentle disposition. She seemed to love my sociability and spontaneity. After a while, though, she tired of my constant social activity and I of her silence. The truism is true: Differences at first attract, and then they divide. The differences that were at first full of mystery and intrigue often come to be regarded with contempt.

True as that is regarding character traits, it is even truer regarding gender. I am very glad to have married a woman—I would have had it no other way. But over time I have wondered many times whether I indeed married a woman or an alien. She is odd, extraordinarily odd.

She wants to snuggle; I want sex. She wants to talk; I want to read. She wants to read; I want to shoot the breeze. She wants sex and I want sex, but somehow even with the same desire, the process seems destined for futility given a dog that is barking two blocks down the road or her concern (which I hear about later) that I've forgotten to change the furnace filter.

Each difference, whether in a matter that is minor or large, seems like the proverbial straw that sinks the boat. And that phrase drives my wife crazy. I can't seem to put aphorisms together right. Is it until the cows fly or pigs? And who cares? My wife cares and she corrects me. Further, if I'm telling a story, say it was two years ago we went to Mt. Rainier, she will add, "No, it was three." Who cares? I'm not in front of a judge, and the point was to note that the trip was not recent yet not in our deep past. It is maddening.

Differences are meant to draw out the part of us that is frightened and repulsed by someone alien and to expose God's delight in the strange and the odd (at least by our estimation). When we are confronted with our ethnocentrism, or more accurately our egocentrism, and how far both are from being God-centered, we are on the precipice of transformation.

God's plan is to allow us to weave a new and unexpected pattern from threads that are different. It is in the new pattern that God begins to demonstrate his love of variety and his joy in our cocreation. Nothing is more monotonous than a weave of one color and one kind of thread. God loves wildness, newness and especially one's influencing another for the sake of the growth of both.

Failure to grow. As a marriage therapist I see this issue as the biggest muddle in most marriages. One spouse wants to grow and the other is resistant, slow or outright opposed. It is the root of enormous heartache and hopelessness in many marriages.

It is unusual, and in fact unlikely, that both partners grow simultaneously at the same rate and with identical trajectories. Growth is more likely to be well paced, even if not identical, if both husband and wife develop a heart to read, pray and talk together regularly about matters that matter. But even reading a book together and doing a Bible study doesn't ensure common, equal growth. That notion ought to go the way of the simultaneous mutual orgasm. It can happen. It is not impossible, but it is as rare as a total eclipse. It is far better to ask: Are we both growing? And is the growth bringing us to more awe, gratitude and joy in our intimacy? If not, then it is possible, if not likely, that there is a failure to grow in the marriage.

Marriages don't grow simply because both spouses age. Growth is intentional, demanding and utterly surprising. It requires space and time. It will not happen without the focus of a gardener who tends, nurtures, weeds, waters, fertilizes and then repeats the same process endlessly. Growth happens because it is desired.

What often happens is that the goal of growing together is given a nod of assent. Husband and wife attend church and perhaps have a minimal spiritual life centered on prayer and reading the Bible. This level of commitment to grow is not to be seen as insignificant, for many couples don't even have this much in common. Those who do, however, seldom set a course for growth. It is the rare couple who will do a conjoint Bible study or attend a weekly group focusing on marriage.

Even fewer couples actually take time to talk about their relationship, dreams, desires, baggage, personal or gender differences, and do so with a heart of openness, curiosity and kindness. It is the rarest of all couples who will then engage in reflection and set goals to grow personally and corporately. In my experience, people let their marriage happen, hope they get along, and utterly ignore the necessity to grow as a person and a couple for the enhancement of the marriage.

In this common scenario, the best counsel that can be given is merely to learn to accept each other as you are without trying to change each other. This means, in fact, get along, kill your desire and don't struggle. If there is little hope for change, if the gospel isn't true, then this counsel is as good as it gets. But if the gospel is true, then heart and relational transformation ought to be the norm and not the rare exception.

THE PLAN

The plan of this book is to consider the matrix of marriage in light of the three commands of Genesis 2:24: leave, weave and cleave. At first we will look closely at what it means to do so and why it is God's design. Then we will consider *how* it is to happen and what happens when we fail to follow God's plan. The goal is simple: to get you thinking about how to grow your marriage in the matrix of his loving plan.

We recommend that as an individual, a couple, a Bible study, growth group or Sunday school class, you read the book and make your way through the companion Bible studies. The studies take the concepts of leave, weave and cleave into the narrative of the characters of the Bible and into other passages that explicate the meaning of Genesis 2:23-25.

The DVD that accompanies the Bible studies presents some of the material through teaching and drama. It is one thing to read of these concepts; it is a whole other matter to see them actually portrayed. We hope you will utilize the fullness of this presentation in all its forms for the glory of your marriage.

A note about pronouns: Throughout this book, the "I" of anecdotes and marriage musings is Dan. Tremper's and my voice unite as "we" in many more general statements. At other times "we" will refer to all of us who struggle, pray and wonder through the muddle of marriage.

It is very hard to hit a target if we don't know where it is. It is nearly impossible to arrive at a desired destination if we are not sure where it is to be found. Simply said, we must know God's goal for our marriage if we are to grow beyond the muddle to discover the meaning he has woven into this relationship. What does God plan for our marriage?

The Meaning of Marriage

No one plans to divorce. No one would consciously stand at the altar saying, "I'll give this a try for a day or two, and if I don't like it, then I'll just get a divorce." Yet many couples begin the divorce process well before the marriage begins. It can happen as simply as both parties believing that a marriage is forever but also highly disposable like a diaper or a used car. Or it can begin soon after the marriage, when one person assumes, *He or she is supposed to make me happy. And if I'm not happy, it is always and fully the other person's fault.*

Marriage, like a journey, can get just a few compass points off, and in a fairly short time it will stray from the path we are meant to follow and miss the destination we are designed to pursue. It may be as simple as this: if you don't know where you are going, you will never arrive. And if you don't know how to get there, then even knowing where you are meant to go will do you little good. We need to know God's destination or goal and the process by which we can arrive there.

THE GOAL OF MARRIAGE

Consider this rather normal interchange between a husband and wife.

HUSBAND: I find you thrilling to the eye and arousing to the touch . . .

WIFE: Are you kidding? Do you know what I've got to get done before the guests arrive? You are mad. You are a raving lunatic.

HUSBAND: Look, I'll help get the house ready, and frankly it won't take forever, and we haven't made love in a week.

WIFE: It won't work to make me feel guilty; plus I expect your help whether we have sex or not.

HUSBAND: Are you saying there's a possibility?

WIFE: Yes, one in a million.

HUSBAND: Excellent, at least there's a chance.

In every interchange between a husband and wife, especially when there is tension, conflict and disagreement, there is the possibility of division. The goal of marriage is intimacy, union, oneness. And at every moment a couple is moving either toward intimacy or away from it.

Obviously there doesn't need to be agreement for intimacy to occur. But it is in the middle of conflict or in moments of potential hurt and disappointment that it is crucial for a couple to know what the goal is— what the abiding and controlling point of marriage is.

Genesis 1—3 gives us a framework and names a number of goals. It is from the matrix of marriage that children are to arise. Children are to be born and grow out of the fundamental fecundity of a loyally committed couple. But the text of Genesis 2 moves us toward a far more relational goal. God says with raw simplicity: It is not good for a man to be alone. Marriage is a union of fundamentally similar beings who couldn't be more different. In the interplay between like and unlike, something occurs that dispels loneliness. That something is what this book is about.

So far the goal of marriage has been named in solely horizontal terms.

From the womb of a marriage we are to have children and to grow an intimacy that banishes or at least minimizes loneliness. It would be unwise to minimize these human dimensions; however, only in the vertical meaning of marriage does the horizontal finds its truest grounding.

Marriage is the human relationship that most reveals the being, character and purpose of God. This key human relationship is designed to make known who God is and how he relates to his world. In marriage we discover who we are, how we are to relate and what we will one day become. The appropriate categories are immense: marriage as *trinity, ethics* and *eschatology*.

Now, most people are bored to tears by theological language because it immediately reminds them of school. We have all spent ghastly hours reading a book or attending a lecture that seems as removed from our day-to-day life as Mars is from Earth. Frankly, who cares? If we are in the middle of a nasty fight with our spouse, we don't care that the way we speak is meant to reveal something about ethics or "the good," or that all our language reflects the promise we made. We just want to know how to get our point across and, if we are honest, to get our spouse to agree.

What difference does it make that marriage is the lens we are to look through to ponder ontology (exploration of the core essence of reality), epistemology (the study of how we know what we know), ethics (the study of how we live out character in relationship) or aesthetics (the study of beauty)? We think it makes all the difference in the world and beyond.

To the professional philosopher or theologian, the claim we have just made is absurd. It is simply not sufficiently academic or intelligent. To the lay reader, it seems too grandiose or abstract. Why bother? It is because marriage is big, really big.

If marriage is indeed the major lens God offers for us to see God's nature and learn how we are to live and what we will one day become, then it is one of the master metaphors to contemplate the enormity of life. When a marriage goes bad, it doesn't just affect a couple, their children and their friends—it is an assault on the very nature of reality, thought and life. Further, if it is accurate to say marriage is this big, then even when we don't fully understand its immensity, we can seek to fathom how marriage is a lens to see well beyond what our naked eye can perceive.

MARRIAGE AS TRINITY

The goal of marriage is to reveal God. And God has revealed himself in Trinity. He is love. He is relationship. He is truth.

The Father, Son and Holy Spirit are coequal in their being and yet reveal their distinctiveness through their different relationships to creation and each other. The Father plans; the Son executes the Father's plan; and the Spirit applies the Son's act in a heart transforming fashion. They are distinct in being, coequal and different in function. Yet they are one God and not three. The mystery is great, but the simple significance is that all truth is at core relational. Truth not only is relational in that it is connected to all other truth, but truth is always revelatory of the heart of God's love for himself and his creation.

It is beyond our comprehension, but the core of all reality, God, is a relational being, that is Trinity. Therefore all things in the universe—cows, unicorns, the second law of thermodynamics, the substratum of the planet Mars, the cure for acid reflux, seminaries, travel agencies, governments, artists, poetry, tractor pulls—are to serve and reflect the ultimate reality of God in and through relationship.

In fact, our ability to know truth is a relational enterprise. We can't know the meaning of $2 + 2 = 4$ outside of a relational matrix. All of our testing of truth and expansion of the true requires a social context to be sensible and meaningful. If God is the core of the universe, then it is no wonder that truth is ultimately a servant of love.

In the above dialogue about sex, the husband is not wrong to want to make love. If he didn't, not only would he be an unusual male, but far worse, he would be divorced from the calling of trinity. A trinitarian view of sex understands that we are meant to merge not merely for physical pleasure but also to enter the great mystery of the many and the one. In the sexual moment a husband and wife enter the holy realm of indwelling, incarnation, flesh and spirit, and the unity and diversity of the Godhead.

Is that meant to make an orgasm better? In some sense yes, but far more, it is meant to help us understand more clearly why evil hates sex—and why God thought of it and loves it. It is intended to help us grasp the importance of asking for sex, wanting sex and engaging honestly and kindly when we don't. It is not so much that sex needs to be elevated so that it becomes more spiritual; it is that sex is meant to be even more important—teaching us, pleasuring us and bringing us a taste of God.

The wife's response is wonderful. She defers by calling the context to mind for both. She prods the husband with the unlikelihood and the silliness of his request. Of course her tone could be punitive and contemptuous, in which case her response violates love. But couples can banter, tease, play and unnerve each other and still remain gracefully in a truthful, kind context.

Desire is not demeaned in this interaction. In honoring desire, we begin to live out a trinitarian view of truth and grace. Desire is what stirs us to ask, seek and knock. It is what sends us on the great journey of life.

Desire is also what usually divides. My desire competes with yours. There are so many pieces of chicken, and I want one more and you do too. We live in a limited, boundary separated, finite world, and the grass on your hill looks greener than mine; your view is more majestic.

The apostle James states it well: "Don't they [fights and quarrels] come from the desires that battle within you?" (James 4:1 NIV). Desire can unite; it usually divides. It can heal, but it usually is the basis of lust and anger, adultery and murder.

Instead I am to emulate the selflessness of the Trinity, rich in desire
and passion, serving each other in perfect unity. I am to be like God. My
marriage is to reflect God.

No wonder desire is either divisive or dead in most marriages. It is
hard to fully and deeply own what we desire and then engage sacrifi-
cially, without selfishness, in serving the other. Marriage is where we discover the truth about the being of God and the truths about our being
as both God-made and good and Fall-stained and dark. Marriage is at
core revelatory.

MARRIAGE AS ETHICS

Marriage not only is revelatory of our failure—this is not hard to
see—but it is also the context for living out the fullness of God's
goodness. We are to be good to each other the way God is good to us.
Marriage is the matrix for *ethics*. Ethics involves the study of what is
a good life and how to live out goodness for others and oneself.

Ethics is pursuit of integrity, honesty, altruism and character. And it is
in marriage that character is most meant to grow. We are characters: each
of us is part of an ongoing story, each is called to know and live out the
part we are to play in the lives of others. We are also endowed with character traits, qualities of goodness that we are to cultivate. We are to grow
in character, becoming more mature in the part we are to play and using
the traits we possess to the glory of God.

Marriage is the soil for us to know and grow our stories, especially our
conjoint story that now brings our pasts together for a new future. In the
midst of this character (persona) development through writing our new
story together, I am to grow a stronger character—an inner disposition
toward integrity.

The growth of my character (persona and inner disposition) comes as
I learn the meaning of my uniqueness—possessing a different gender,
background, history, abilities, struggles—and use that uniqueness to

serve the good of my spouse. What if the husband who is asking for sex has a history of being abused sexually? Probably more risk and shame are attached to his request than would be to a similar request by a man who has not suffered that harm. What if the wife he asks has had a tragic history of past immorality, where her body was a commodity and she violated herself using sex as a tool rather than as an expression of intimacy? Her turning down sex may have more to do with contempt for her husband and her own body than it might if immorality had not been a part of her story.

How do we live out the character we are for the other and grow to have a stronger character as an individual? This involves the difficult question of what is the "good" life. Does it lie in being a missionary? Having lots of money? Being successful in one's career? Doing lots of community service? Having lots of friends? Going to church? Owning one's own home? Being hip, cool and living on the edge? Good at sports? Thin? Saving for retirement? Reading the *Wall Street Journal*?

Whether we know it or not, we are constructing our version of the good life every time we make a decision to read the *Wall Street Journal* versus the *National Enquirer,* or to watch a reality show rather than practice Spanish. Whether we are a duffer who hacks away at golf or a limber practitioner of Hatha Yoga, we are choosing what we perceive to be the good in order to live well. Even when we know we are being unethical or unloving, we are still involved in an ethical pursuit of what we call "good."

Marriage is a crucial matrix where we experiment and refine how we will live ethically. If we cheat on our wife, we will cheat in every other arena of life. If we are faithful to our spouse, it doesn't mean we will live well elsewhere, but it is at least a good bet that we will. Marriage is the beginning point of how we construct our character for the world. In the womb of this relationship, God intends for us to craft our character to be like his own.

MARRIAGE AS ESCHATOLOGY

The goal of marriage is trinitarian, to grow relationship, and ethical, to grow character. But both goals are in service to the greatest goal: making God known. Marriage is a foretaste, a hors d'oeuvre of what will one day be our ultimate joy—being with God in intimate relationship forever. That is called the climax of history, the consummation.

It is not too surprising that the last day of the present world system and all that follows is referred to in sexual terms. What metaphor other than intercourse and orgasm could possibly denote the completeness and ecstasy of the eschaton? And not only ecstatic pleasure is denoted by the notion of climax and consummation—marriage is also meant to be a picture of sabbath rest. A good marriage is a rousing, joyous, sensuous celebration and a good, long, cozy nap.

The Bible pictures the end of all things as the wedding feast of the Lamb. In this day every tear will be wiped away and all suffering due to sin will be obliterated. Evil will be destroyed, never again to be present for all eternity. It is a day of food and sex, a day of desire fulfilled and new, holy, fully redeemed desire set free.

It is utterly impossible to imagine in concrete terms what that day will hold. It is ridiculous to try to picture what we will do for an hour, or for that matter whether the passage of time will have any meaning. All we can do to speak of that day is to lay hyperbole like aromatic mustard on the best of what this world holds for us. It will be like the best surprise party, homecoming, wedding, banquet that we've ever experienced or imagined—and then more. So much more that it misses the point to try to capture it by saying it will be like a hole in one, landing the biggest trout of one's life, selling a million books or getting the best hug you've ever received from your daughter. All of life points toward that moment, but nothing points more clearly toward the consummation than sexual climax.

Of course that is an orgasm, but it would be a big mistake to conclude that sex is to be equated with an orgasm. Sex is gender. Sex is an engendered body relating to another (trinity) in order to grow one's heart and character (ethics). Sex is a man and a woman touching on every level—spiritually, relationally, physically—in order to grow wonder and joy, awe and gratitude, and these in turn lead us to say to God, "I praise you; your creation is bone of my bone, flesh of my flesh, and it is good."

Marriage is the promise of a day in which the pain of our failures will be wiped away. We will be full, flaming holy beauty that lives and moves to serve the King of Kings. Meanwhile, today I get to love my wife, hold her hand, feel the pulse of her wild and gorgeous heart, and feel alive, sensual, erotic, bold, full and brave as I protect and provide for her body and soul.

I get to do so with the promise that no matter how well or how badly we are doing today, there will be a tomorrow. That tomorrow will one day shine so bright and full that all I've suffered today will seem a light and momentary suffering. Marriage is a ground of suffering and redemption. Salvation must be true in marriage or it is not true at all. Marriage must be the place where hope grows, or there is no reason to hope. It is a window into the coming kingdom of God.

MARRIAGE AS REVELATION

Marriage is meant to be a space where the most holy and intimate God shows himself as compelling and good. It is meant to work—not easy, not always and not without his presence. Nonetheless, marriage is meant to be a relationship that shouts to the world: "He is glorious and good!"

How is that message to be fashioned? What is the safe womb, the plan, we are to follow? The next chapter will look at the matrix of marriage found in the plan: leave your mother and father, weave intimacy with your spouse, and cleave to one another to know the passion of God.

THREE

The Matrix of Marriage

Marriages are ending at an unprecedented rate. In the United States the rate has generally been over 50 percent, but among folks between the ages of twenty-five and thirty-five the rate is up to 60 percent. It is staggering. Consider this: if you knew that one out of every two planes would crash, I doubt you would travel by air. And if one out of every two times you went to a restaurant you got food poisoning, I seriously think you would only eat at home.

Then why do people continue to walk the aisle sporting a huge grin, anticipating a life of bliss? We believe the answer is simple: it is the relationship that most mirrors the Garden of Eden and reflects our desire for true and lasting intimacy.

Marriages, more than ever, are troubled and need a safe place. We need to let our marriage grow in God's plan. In his hand we can grow into the fullness of a reflection of him. God has created a process in which marriages can prosper, and it is in the simple plan of Genesis 2:24:

- leave all past loyalties
- weave hearts through communion
- unite (cleave) in sensual/physical oneness

Often Genesis 2:24 has been cited as God's plan for marriage. It is that. Genesis 2:24 has further been called a blueprint or a roadmap according to which a marriage is to be lived. That is not accurate, at least not as most people would use a map or a blueprint.

God doesn't tell us *how* to leave, just to do so. He doesn't give a hint as to how to interweave two hearts, nor what is involved in becoming one flesh. He simply states that this is to happen.

God's plan is the *telos*, the end point, to which we are to travel; it is also the beginning point from which we are to move. It is as if God said, "The goal of marriage is intimacy. Now find the route you are to travel to get there. But as you go, remember to trust me. Don't stop until you arrive at true joy. The journey will take you places you never dreamed."

A thousand routes may take us to the same end. Is that a blueprint? Is that a roadmap?

The point is simple. Marriage has a form to be lived, and yet the structure could be quite simple or quite complex. For this reason we do better to use the metaphor of a *matrix,* a womb, a safe place where marriage is incubated and grows in order to travel to the place God has designed.

What difference does a metaphor make? The difference is enormous. With the metaphor of a matrix rather than a blueprint, I feel much less pressure to figure out exactly the "right way" to leave my mother and father. The issue is not trying to "do it right," because God refuses in this instance to give me a standard set of steps to follow. On the other hand, having freedom can be unnerving. I don't need to figure out how to do it *right,* but I am called to ponder how to do it *well.* The difference between *right* and *well* implies wholeness, a fullness of response, rather than a performance of compliance.

I am called to ponder what God's call means not for all couples, not as a universal that is to be lived out identically in every marriage, but for my marriage, our marriage. I am to create and not merely obey. Indeed, I am to obey by creating. Every marriage on the earth from time immemorial calls a couple to grow in the matrix of God's plan—creatively, uniquely and collaboratively. We are given a nest in which to grow, and eventually we are leave the nest as we grow up in the pursuit of what a marriage (or life) is meant to become.

THE MATRIX

> This explains why a man leaves his father and mother and is joined to his wife, and the two are united into one.
>
> Now the man and his wife were both naked, but they felt no shame. (Genesis 2:24-25)

Leave: A communion of faith. The Bible's call to leave or to depart from past loyalty to one's parents has no parallels in ancient Near Eastern literature. It is no less radical in our culture and time. To leave is to place a boundary between ourselves and the people, customs, influences and baggage that once defined who we are. It is a call to a new beginning.

Relationships grow in the soil of trust. And the most important relationship, marriage, is designed to require a trust unlike any other. All relationships require trust, but a marriage requires a level of trust that is unprecedented. It requires a radical surrender to the future through an abandonment of the past.

The departure is neither fundamentally physical nor financial, but psychological. In the ancient Near East a couple's leaving would not have been geographical, for extended families lived together under the same roof or in the same compound. Leaving would not have been financial, since extended families made their living on common land and usually within the same guild. The departure would have to do with identity: *Who am I? Who are we?*

The new identity would be as a distinct, wholly different family that owes its fundamental loyalty to itself and its children and not to grandparents, parents, siblings or other extended family.

This is a beautiful and complex calling. We are no longer to lean on our families nor allow them to occupy the matrix of our marriage. It doesn't mean that our parents and our past are cut off and thrown away; it simply calls each new couple to cocoon for a time to establish their own order and ethos.

Leaving requires a couple to build a boundary, to have at least a door with a lock. And then it demands that each spouse learn to say no to invitations and demands of the outside world, especially one's own parents.

Once a boundary is set—the door is solid and lockable and the freedom to say no is well established—the couple can furnish their home by drawing from the customs and traditions, the invitations and requests, and the expectations, both direct and indirect, that come from outside.

If this doesn't occur, then inevitably someone other than the husband and wife will make the decisions about how their home will be furnished. Often it will be the most dominant or powerful parent. It really doesn't matter who it is: the effect will be the same—an erosion of trust.

How can I trust you when you let your mother divide us? How can I trust you when your father tells us what we are to do? The issue is loyalty. Will you live and die for me, or are you bound to an empty pursuit of your parent's blessing? If it is the latter, then I know it is not love that rules you but fear. And if it is fear of displeasure, then I know your heart is not warmed by love but shaped by the fear of rejection. A new spouse knows that when the novelty of new love wears thin, blood is thicker than water.

The result will be that something is held back, and I cushion the call to trust, to surrender to the other, by leaning a little more back toward my parents and past. If you are unwilling to let go, then I too must not fully abandon myself to this new relationship. The marriage is divided. Over time the division will inevitably grow. Trust will be eroded. Pain will grow. Disappointment will turn to bitterness. The whole mess will usually be quarantined into a demilitarized zone (DMZ) that walls away issues that cannot be addressed without starting a war. From the beginning the marriage is slowly moving toward distance or divorce.

Weave: A communion of hope. A new marriage is meant to build a strong, permeable but highly resistant barrier between itself and the world. Once there is space and safety to grow, the couple is meant to talk. It is through the medium of words, the Word, the Logos (Jesus), that intimacy grows.

Picture being in an off-the-beaten-path cabin, with snow piled high outside, a roaring fire inside, plenty of provisions and time to be together. Now what would you do? If the answer is to check your e-mail, finish a project or play computer games, shoot yourself! If it is to call up a friend because you're bored, then you know something is desperately wrong. If your answer is to snuggle and giggle and roll up the bear rug around two naked bodies, then you can at least pass go and collect two hundred dollars. But what happened before and after the naked play?

Verbal intercourse is meant to lead eventually to the fires of sexual play. But where there is a dearth of conversation, or a drone of words but little meaningful talk, there will always be a sense of sexual emptiness, no matter how good the sex. Talk is the lubricant of sex.

A couple at the wedding altar makes a series of promises. These vows are meant to be the verbal boundaries that guide all conversations, decisions and life directions. It is odd that we don't stitch the words onto our shirts or emblazon them on our ceiling so they are the first thing we see when we awaken and the last words we read before we sleep. Instead, most couples wouldn't remember what they promised if asked at their wedding reception.

Words are a promise. Words are always an investment in the future. Consider something as simple as this exchange.

HUSBAND: I am going to run into town. Do you need anything?

WIFE: No, but if you can wait an hour I'd love to go with you.

HUSBAND: Shoot, I really need to go now if I am going to get the part
           for the sink before the hardware store closes.

WIFE: Okay. Well, at least let's take a walk after you get back.

This is an oath-grounded, promise-keeping, normal interchange. He informs and submits his plan to her desires or needs. She answers and graces him with the desire to be with him. He acknowledges some disappointment but chooses not to do as she wishes. She in turn acknowledges the priority to go now, but she looks to the future to bring them to a point of connection.

The husband doesn't directly say, "Trust me, I will not cheat on you when I go to town." Nor does the couple even say, "I love you." Nonetheless, there is promise and loyalty-keeping depth to their interplay. Words are meant to highlight the boundaries already set and then to create what has yet to be formed.

This happens when we go to a movie and spend an hour afterward talking about the characters, the plot, the ending and what it all means to us. Or when I am reading a book and have to read a paragraph aloud to my wife, even if we have little conversation about what I read. Such conversation is the creation of ideas, plans and dreams. It is allowing words to be an imaginary path on which we walk before we plunge into the maelstrom of reality. It is talk—but talk that links our hearts because we speak with freedom, confidence and pleasure in a way we could not and should not speak to any other.

The heartache of many marriages is that it is easier to have a meaningful, curious, playful discussion with a stranger on a plane than with one's own spouse. This is a form of infidelity. If you are married to a silent, angry, critical or contemptuous person, it is inevitable that you will have more meaningful conversations with people at work or strangers on airplanes than with your own spouse.

Often this tragedy comes because of a failure to leave one's parents and past. It can also arise due to a failure to bless the differences between the two. A woman talks, thinks, feels and is different from a man; a man is different from a woman in these same ways. We are written by God to be a reflection of his image, and his character is said to be equally strong and tender. A man is more typically strong and a woman more tender. This is not mere socialization but the hardwiring of God's creation. Sadly, the differences that should unite us are rather allowed to divide us. They often provoke contempt and not wonder.

A couple must cleave—be united in heart and soul, in word and deed—to honor and learn and grow from the distinctiveness of each other. As we do so, God invites us to become one flesh.

Cleave: A communion of love. To become one flesh righteously before God is an investment of discipline and diligence. It is an issue of loyalty. During our courtship I will honor God and I will honor you by choosing to put a boundary between us, at the very time we are putting boundaries between ourselves and all other suitors and even our parents and friends.

The complexity of sexual struggle at this point is a precursor for setting boundaries in the future. If I am not faithful to honor your body and mine during our courtship, how can you have confidence and trust that I will honor my vows of purity in the future? Sexual joy depends on a boundary-making loyalty and a promise of word that is written in deeds of blood and bone.

And most couples fail, even if not to the extent of having intercourse. Most couples "go too far," whatever that means. The result is a residue of resentment, hurt, disappointment, blame and shame that often doesn't circulate through the house until sexual intensity begins to wane, after honeymoon bliss is eclipsed by the problems of work and the presence of children. The guarantee in marriage is that sex will not begin well and simply get better. For every honest couple, sex is a roller-coaster ride of ups and downs, ecstasy and boredom, success and failure.

No wonder God calls us to first leave and grow in trust and then commune in word to develop heart-to-heart intimacy. We need such faith and hope to grow the passion of love. And sex is love, even if love is not sex.

Sex is the physical, sensual manifestation of the intangible presence of love. Sex, as erotic play, is as different for a man and a woman as communication is. If men and women talk differently—and they do—then it should come as no surprise that God has hardwired their bodies to respond differently.

A man is primed to respond to sight and to do so with focus, intensity and speed. A woman responds to relational cues and does so with a more diffuse, relaxed and slow engagement. We are the same and opposite. This leads to a huge potential for conflict and contempt.

God's plan sexually is that one must surrender (leave) to the dialogue (weave) of sensually serving the other (love) in order to know the greatest pleasure for oneself (ecstasy). It is just brilliant. Serving another is not annihilating or neglecting yourself; in fact, it is the only righteous way to enjoy being who God wrote you to be.

Sex is in that sense equivalent to the Lord's Table. We are to eat the bread and wine to remember him—to worship and serve him. But in so doing we are given the earthly, sensual elements of life we need to be nourished, strong and alive. The same is true for our sexual joy with our spouse. Sex is a sensual symbol, a metaphor with skin that gives us a window into the wonder of God's heart and plan.

It should be no surprise that evil hates sex and wishes to ruin it. Nor should it surprise us that shame has come to be bound to our sexuality. But in facing the effects of shame and its shadow of heartache, we are called to enter more richly and fully into communion with our forgiving and healing God. Sex ought to drive us back again and again into the arms of our lover God. His embrace frees us to delight in the touch of our spouse. Simply said, marriage prods us to seek a deeper relationship with our God.

Leaving

Making Space for Faithfulness

This explains why a man leaves his father and mother
and is joined to his wife, and the two are united
into one.

Now the man and his wife were both naked, but they
felt no shame.

GENESIS 2:24-25

I could see my wife's eyes as she read a section of another writing project. She was not impressed. She was either irritated or bored, or both. I thought maybe I shouldn't ask, but eventually curiosity prevailed and I said, "Well, what did you think of the chapter?"

She replied, "I am not your greatest fan, you know."

I should have fled from the conversation, if not the house, but foolishly I pressed on. "What didn't you like? Is it too negative or just unclear? What's wrong with it?"

She looked at me and smiled a captivating and radiant smile. She shrugged and said, "I am just not interested in the things you write, and this chapter in particular bored me."

I wanted to scream or yell, but I took her offhand global critique in stride and asked, "What are we having for dinner?"

My wife will be bored by my analysis of the conversation, but I found it disturbing and hopeful. The potential for division and hurt was huge. She was critiquing not merely my writing but my whole career and life focus. I am in love with a woman who is not a fan of my writing or of therapy. She sees life from a different standpoint, and we often clash about matters large and small. But I trust her opinion about my writing and most other issues. I solicit her feedback about complex psychological matters, and even when she is bored I find her fascinating.

The reason we can bear disruption and endure one another's radically different opinions is that we trust each other. Trust is a gift that is more valuable than gold and rare as a twenty-karat diamond. Trust in a marriage can be shattered through an affair, lies and deceit. It can be eroded over decades as one simply forgets to prize the other more than all else in life. But trust can never truly be established in the beginning unless a couple severs the bonds of loyalty with their parents, past, possessions and power.

A husband and wife are to leave their mother and their father—and by implication all other loyalties—in order to create space for a new trust to grow without the entanglement of old loyalties. It is the first command for marriage, and when it is violated or ignored, a marriage is doomed to be less than it was meant to be and will wither and fail to produce good fruit.

LEAVING FOR GOOD AND FOR GOD

Leaving implies a departure from the comfort and safety of a home in which I am neither an owner nor a guest. In the ancient Near East a child was an heir but not on equal footing with regard to the rights and privileges of a parent. Nor was a child considered to be a guest. A guest in that time was even more honored and protected than a child or relative of the host. A guest would be offered the best of one's food and wine and accorded protection; the host was obligated to care for the guest as long as he or she stayed under the host's roof.

A child, on the other hand, was loved but accorded value often on the basis of birth order and gender. A second son had less inherent value than the first, and a girl always was less important than a boy. Children were esteemed to the degree that they brought joy to their parents and did nothing that would bring disgrace to their family name. Their value lay in honoring their parents and working for their family's well-being. There was not a great deal of ground for individuality or freedom of choice. Life was fairly closely dictated by the family cult, tribal customs and the weekly and seasonal celebrations at the temple.

A young man or woman would be given to marriage between the ages fourteen and eighteen. Marriages were arranged; marrying for love was not a common theme or custom. Being given in marriage meant being betrothed for nearly a year, after which the couple would consummate their relationship. More often than not the couple lived with the groom's parents and remained under their wing and provision for years if not for a lifetime. It is within this culture that God insists a couple must leave their mother and father.

As noted earlier, couples in that culture did not make a departure that was geographical or financial. Rather, leaving was a division that implied a degree of privacy and primacy. In the sprawling, open architecture of that time and place, a young couple was to have their own room shared by no one else in the family. They were to be alone. And not only were they to enjoy a measure of privacy, the relationship was to be given a primacy that supplanted all other commitments and loyalties—even to one's own parents.

We are commanded to honor our parents, but honoring is never to be assumed to be more important than leaving. In fact, the command to honor is given well after the initial call for a man and women to depart from the authority of their parents. We can honor our mother and father only if we have first created the proper boundary to serve and protect our spouse.

Honoring our mother and father is not a command to avoid honesty, conflict or disagreement. Many take it as a demand to make sure a parent is never unhappy. But God didn't put that kind of pressure or responsibility on children. To honor is to acknowledge with gratitude the gift of life we have been given through our parents. It is to name with joy who we have become due to their failures and glory.

Ultimately, honoring is a tangible way of thanking God for the provision he has offered us through our parents. We are to honor parents who were phenomenal and those who were evil. In either case, we can name what is true, bless them for what we've learned and become, and invite them to grow to become even more who they were meant to be. But the growth of our parents is not our first calling.

Our first calling as a married person is to bring pleasure to our spouse. The book of Deuteronomy gives this counsel not only to newlyweds but to the authorities of the civil government and the military: "A newly married man must not be drafted into the army or be given any other official responsibilities. He must be free to spend one year at home, bringing happiness to the wife he has married" (Deuteronomy 24:5).

Pleasure includes everything from companionship to good sex. Woe to a ruler or commander or parent who gets in the way of good sex! A new relationship needs time and safety to grow as a young, insecure shoot. Only by building a boundary against the past can a couple be relatively safe from harm.

BOUNDARY BUILDING
Boundaries are acknowledgments of the inevitability of dispute, divi-

sion and danger. If I don't mark my property line, eventually the owner of the adjacent property will presume that my land is under his or her ownership. It is best to build a wall along the property line as a means of settling a dispute before it arises. If the line is held in agreement, then we have kept a dispute from dividing us and throwing us into a war of words or stones.

The book of Proverbs warns us: "Don't cheat your neighbor by moving the ancient boundary markers; /don't take the land of defenseless orphans. /For their Redeemer is strong; /he himself will bring their charges against you" (Proverbs 23:10-11). The counsel is not just offered with regard to land disputes. We are to honor the boundaries of a marriage. According to the Ten Commandments we are to honor the boundaries of our parents (commandment 5), life itself (commandment 6), another person's spouse (commandment 7), personal property (commandment 8), reputation and truth (commandment 9), and separate ourselves from lust and envy (commandment 10). In fact, the Ten Commandments are built on creating a boundary between the true God and all others who would claim to be god (commandment 1). From the first, the commandments with regard to graven images, oaths of loyalty and the creation of a day of rest arise because of a commitment to separate or mark off space that is not ours in order to honor what God has given us to treasure and protect. Boundaries honor God, others and our marriage.

Boundaries mark off space not to cut off contact with others but to protect the young trust that is beginning to take root. Note this well: jealous, possessive boundary building that cuts a person off from their family, friends, customs and care is *not biblical.* It is abusive and violating, and inevitably it becomes the basis of some form of domestic violence. No spouse should ever be severed from their family and friends under the guise of leaving all past loyalties. No spouse should ever pressure a young wife or husband with the words "It is either them or me!" If your spouse seeks to force you to make such a choice, it is wise to seek counseling and pastoral care. In most healthy relationships, the design of boundaries always includes a passageway—a doorway in the wall or a ladder to comfortably climb over the wall.

The point of boundary building is to honor the necessity to grow a new trust without undue intrusions or complications. Boundaries are to be built not only with our family, siblings, relatives and friends but also with regard to our past. We are to create a new boundary in relation to old boyfriends or girlfriends; sports, hunting and fishing buddies; neighbors and work colleagues. When we get married, it is like becoming a Christian: all things become new. And all things will change.

The changes need not be surgically intense and quick, but they need to be planned for and brought about with thoughtful and intentional speed. Leaving doesn't require us to totally give up all we believed and did and cared about in the past—but it does call both husband and wife to the high commitment to be willing to give up anything and everything for the sake of the marriage. Now you must be open to changing everything, yet if your spouse *requires* you to do so, then it is both dangerous and wrong. The principle instead is to hold loosely to all one was while the task of forming a new world together takes priority over the pleasures and predictability of the past.

As in most matters of the heart, the issue is not what we do as much as what we desire for the sake of the other. Imagine that I say to my young bride, "But I've always gone bowling on Tuesday nights. I'll be home by 11 p.m., and it's just my night out with the guys." If my spouse resents my bowling, I need to take her concerns seriously. The appropriate response to her concerns, however, is not an immediate decision to never bowl again. It may mean postponing being on my team for six months. That decision may cost me friendships or a place on a championship team.

And still the decision is not finished once I'm willing to sacrifice my bowling night for a time. Questions must be asked of my wife: What is it that you fear? What is it you most desire? How can we bless each other even when there are strong and deep differences between us?

A spouse who stops doing something for no reason except that the other has requested it will likely harbor resentment for the demand and feel weak for their choice to avoid conflict. The resulting anger mixed with self-contempt is a deadly combination that is more treacherous than carbon monoxide. It is better to make no quick decision but to engage in a dialogue that will deepen respect for each other and oneself and lead to a mutually chosen decision.

Leaving also involves a clean and deep division from anything or anyone that might harm our love. Such dangers are too many to name comprehensively. They include but are not limited to all past loves, addictions, sexual history, sexual abuse, and the paraphernalia and baggage of our past wounds. (If you need to, it would be most honorable to take a gulp and read that last sentence again.)

As a therapist I have worked with many who have been married for twenty years and still never addressed the hold that past relationships or sin have on the marriage. Often a young spouse will hide incriminating struggles like sexual addiction, a lust for pornography or other sexual sins, hoping they will melt away in the presence of legal, God-honoring marital sex. Sadly, they don't. Often only years later does their spouse discover an "affair" involving pornography and masturbation. In a violently promiscuous world, such sins may seem almost innocuous, but I have never worked with an honest woman who did not suffer significant betrayal from so-called minor failures.

The fact is, the past is full of memories and tragedies that are easier to bury than to name and face. Yet note well that we are *not* saying to a young couple, "Don't get married until you've resolved all the struggles of your past so that you don't bring any baggage into the new relationship." If we were to attempt such a resolution, no one would ever be married, because none of us are ever finished longing for redemption for our past.

It seems complicated, but the core issue is again quite simple: am I more loyal to my shame by hiding my past than I am to opening my heart to my spouse or spouse-to-be? It is not that I must "resolve" all my past, it is that I need to be able to say yes to this question: am I open, in due season, to letting my spouse walk through the heartache of the past for the sake of redemption?

Anything that might compromise the opening of our hearts to each other needs to be left behind. This opens both hearts to the invitation to be intimate allies.

INVITING TRUST

The value of trust in a marriage is inestimable. The result of an absence of trust is highly calculable: division and/or divorce. A marriage without trust is an empty well—it promises satisfaction but it never delivers. In turn it leads to suspicion, cynicism and contempt. It is poisonous and over time withers both parties to a fraction of their humanity.

Gollum in the Lord of the Rings films gives us an image of the withering, dehumanizing power of jealous mistrust. Gollum valued nothing in life more than the golden Ring of Power. He gave up his "humanity"—in his case hobbithood—because he loved power more than care. Trust always involves putting one's pursuit of power or joy aside for the sake of another.

The word *trust* comes from the English word *troth*. Troth means truth. To trust another person is to count them as a person who loves the truth. It is not merely a matter of being honest; it is being a person who loves integrity and can admit when truth is lacking in their life.

What a difference it makes to feel safe. Trust clears away all the boulders and stumps that would keep one's field from being fruitful. It sets the boundaries to ensure the ground is honored and protected. And then trust invites the other to play.

If you watch children who are awkward and unsure of their environment, you will see the power of mistrust. They are on edge and never able to relax; their movements are jerky and nervous. The tenser one feels, the more cautious and watchful one becomes. The body's feedback loop reads the tension, and the natural tendency of fight or flight increases. Then even a small problem is escalated into a huge issue. Anger and anxiety always accompany mistrust. The byproduct is obvious—the more mistrust, the greater the potential for division.

Trust is not a byproduct of love; it doesn't grow on the same vine. Love as agape is without condition. It is offered without cause; therefore it cannot be earned or lost. But trust is a different fruit. It is *earned* over a lifetime.

It is imperative to consider the implications of that statement. *Trust is earned over a lifetime through small moments of faithfulness.*

Jesus states: "Because you have been trustworthy in a very small matter, take charge of ten cities" (Luke 19:17 NIV). The assumption is that we earn our way to greater authority and privilege.

We must never presume that a marriage has either enough trust or enough love. Both are to grow over a lifetime, but love can't flourish in its playful, free and tender offering unless trust is solid and sure. In that sense, trust is the foundation of a marriage, whereas love becomes the home where we find shelter and warmth.

My wife and I had been married for nineteen years when she told me a story from her childhood. It was a sad story of being made fun of in fourth grade. Her experience was not horrific or unique—probably most of us have suffered such cruelty sometime during elementary school—but I was heartbroken. I wanted to wrap her up in my arms and wipe away her tears. I wanted to make the girls who had mocked her pay for eternity.

After we had talked about the implications of the experience, it dawned on me that I had never heard the story before, and I asked why it had come up at this point. I was asking: What prompted the story now?

My wife heard the question from a different perspective. She heard: What has enabled you to tell me the story now? She replied, "I trust you now in a way I didn't a year ago."

I was stunned. At first I felt hurt. How could she say she didn't trust me? Then I began to ponder, *What has happened in a year to permit that story to rise to the surface?* I had no answer, so I asked.

My wife's response was peculiar. She said, "I don't know, but I do know you are more open to hurt for me rather than try to fix me."

I had never perceived of myself as a Mr. Fix-It Man, but apparently in the jumble of tens of thousands of interactions I had distinguished myself more as a helper than as a healer. My wife wanted me to enter her story and not fix it. Somehow over that year she had seen the tumult of my life alter my way of relating to her. The fixing problem had never been named, but it was a "small" thing that had to be transformed before my wife could entrust me with the "bigger" stories of her life.

A husband or wife ought not be offended to find that trust is not full or finished. To put it more dramatically: no one should be surprised or upset that trust is mixed with mistrust. A wife might say, "I trust my husband until he's at a fishing expo, and then I know he is going to buy junk he doesn't need. He just loses his head." Many husbands can say, "I trust my wife, but when she is with her sister I know things will be said that I have begged her not to say. She just can't help herself."

Trust is earned, and earned the hard way—day to day, in the small matters, through intentional movements of truth-loving deeds.

Leaving

Walking Away from Home

Cars need tending. Not long ago our family car decided it had been abandoned long enough and unless it smoked and fumed I would never care for it. That was accurate.

Sitting at a stoplight, I could smell something that combined plaintive with putrid. It was the smell of an engine starting to seize and die. I had enough wisdom to turn the engine off and check the oil. Due to random luck, I eventually found what often is called the dip stick and discovered the car had not been fed in many moons. We averted a tragedy, but only by the slim molecules of a few drops of oil.

If something mechanical like a car needs care and nourishment, then obviously so does a living entity like a plant, and even more a relationship. Trust is grown through labor as painstaking as that required for tending a vineyard. Trust is a sweet and nourishing fruit that requires daily care. If left unattended, not only will the vineyard not grow good fruit, but it will be overwhelmed in a short time by weeds.

"Leaving" is not a onetime event that is completed when you no longer live near your parents or receive their financial support. Leaving creates the ground for trust to grow by circumventing intrusions or dangers that could spread wild seed and destroy good fruit.

This chapter will explore how a couple is to leave one's parents and past. The purpose is twofold. (1) For those who are young in their marriage, the goal is to encourage deliberate early decisions to build honoring boundaries. (2) For those who are older in their marriage and may have failed to leave as God desires, the goal is to consider how to rebuild trust based on a never-too-late departure.

The good news is that trust is secured to a strong and vibrant vine—the faithfulness of God. No marriage is secure that fails to put its roots in God. But with God's help, even the most devastating rupture of trust can over time be healed, and so it is never too late to bind our branches into his vine. The only error is to believe that trust is a given and is secure simply because a marriage has lasted a number of years.

WALKING AWAY FROM OUR FAMILIES

The previous chapter made it clear that departing from our family doesn't mean severing family bonds. Such a rupture would be required only after repeated efforts to address the harm caused by a parent who perpetrates incontrovertibly soul-demeaning, dignity-denigrating acts of harm. We are to remain involved with parents who have not been guilty of such egregious evil. Nonetheless, we are still called to "leave" them. Leaving involves creating a space where privacy, primacy and power are in the hands of the couple and not their families of origin.

Privacy. Maintaining privacy involves far more than requiring family members to ring the doorbell before they enter our home. Privacy holds all matters of intimacy in confidentiality. It implies that whatever would cause embarrassment or shame if revealed is kept private. How you sing in the shower might not be a matter of huge embarrassment, but why would I tell a group of our friends that you warble like an idling diesel? Life is so complex—in fact, it might be slightly embarrassing to tell how you sing, but it would be a matter of mutual joy that your passion for life is so robust in the morning. I don't know what to tell or not to tell until I've gotten to know you through trial and error—in other words, through failure.

A theme that will be struck many times through this chapter is that trust is grown primarily through repair of its violation. If we labor simply to avoid failure, the cost is a cautious, labored life. It is better to ask forgiveness than permission. It is even better to live with a daily, profound awareness that without the capacity to humble oneself, to ask for and to embrace forgiveness, trust has no capacity to grow in a marriage.

This message needs to be underlined. I am not talking about cavalier failure that is patched up with a perfunctory "I'm sorry, please forgive me." Such sniveling misuse of the gospel is not only cheap grace; it is no grace at all. Failure is inevitable, and it ought to break our heart when we defraud or violate our partner for life.

Honoring privacy will become even more crucial when a spouse says, "Please don't share this with your mother." It is now not a question of being better to ask forgiveness than permission. It is now a matter of honor and integrity. If a spouse can't keep secrets, the marriage can't last.

The heartache of confidentiality is that a secret, like money, burns in our pocket. It is there to be spent, and to "save" it leaves the heart feeling empty. The soul must grow if it is to bear the discomfort. But by holding a secret in a place of honor, we show ourselves not only committed but strong enough to be trusted in other matters.

Primacy. Leaving one's parents establishes the primacy of the marriage over all other relationships. Marriage is meant to be a statement: "I forsake all others for the sake of you." And this will be tested at its nadir during the preparations for the wedding. The classic archetype is the dyadic nightmare of the mother of the bride and the wedding planner. What ought to be a relatively simple and inexpensive process becomes the signature event of one's life to prove one's personal success, good breeding and familial power. Planning such a wedding is like crossing a bog infested with crocodiles and a whole Satanic host. The wise course is to elope. (Of course I don't actually believe that is best, until as a father of two daughters I consider the terrifying prospect of paying for two major-production weddings.)

If for the sake of personal preference and future with one's in-laws and parents elopement is not chosen, then primacy will be conditioned, challenged and banged up from the get-go. Unless, of course, the parents of both bride and groom are mature enough to let them plan the vast majority of the event.

It is wisdom to enjoy the day no matter how crazy it becomes. Let the leaving begin with just a few decisions regarding the event; the rest can be determined, as needed, by the wedding planner and the obligations of one's culture.

After the ceremony, flee. The honeymoon has little to do with a great vacation and good sex. Both are nice, but the real meaning of the honeymoon is to get away. In our culture, primacy is evidenced in the quality of the ring and the honeymoon. I failed at both: I gave my wife a diamond that was smaller than a mustard seed, and we honeymooned at a free cabin without running water on Cold Mountain during the coldest winter in North Carolina's history. I have a forgiving wife, but several karats and Hawaii winter vacations later have not hurt our subsequent relationship. It is better, far better, to begin well rather than try to make up later for a lame start.

The issue of primacy surfaces early, but the big events do not matter as much as what can seem somewhat inconsequential. The rub comes in how you handle decisions where the desires of your family are at odds with those of your spouse. Where will we spend the first or twentieth Christmas? Whose family name will mark the first grandson? Will you move for a job or remain close to your family? Will you visit parents on your vacation or take an actual vacation? Countless issues from dinner dates, holidays, money, phone calls, to not talking politics, religion, markets or childrearing are fraught with the potential for division.

What happens is that peace tends to be valued over primacy. Peace holds the promise that someday I will get my parent's or parent-in-law's blessing. The hope in the heart of every child is one day a parent will crown us with a good word that calls us to be all we are meant to be. Such a word goes far beyond an affirmation or mere encouragement. It is a blessing—a naming of heart, gift and calling. One takes such an inheritance into the dark and unsure days as a surety of goodness. We fear we will not receive a blessing if we are independent and fail at doing what our parents desire.

I never received a blessing from my father. And it hurts. Whether we are aware of the desire or deny it outright as quaint or unnecessary, it is built into our heart. We are often willing, though unwittingly so, to sacrifice our spouse for the sake of retaining order, ease and connection with our parents in the hope that the blessing will someday be given.

The sacrifice often happens in a subtle and passing moment. A parent says, "Oh dear, I don't want you to trouble your husband/wife, but I think it would be very distressing if you all didn't come home sometime this summer. Now don't bring this up to your father—he would deny it—but I know it will kill him if you don't come home." Mom has just set a terrible trap. She has required primacy with her on three counts: (1) don't tell your wife/husband, (2) arrange your summer to visit your parents, and (3) don't tell your father that she asked.

Her intentions may be golden, but her method is snakelike. She is deceptive and manipulative. To bow to her control is not merely to lose your integrity; it violates a commitment to honor your spouse above all others. This is true even if your spouse *wants* to visit your parents over the summer. The issue is not whether you arrange your summer vacation to go home or not; it is the issue of primacy. The best response is simple: "Oh Mom, thanks for the offer. I will talk with Jenny to let her know of your concern and then with Dad, and afterward I will let you know what we'll choose."

Primacy means that the only secrets kept are between husband and wife; there are none between a spouse and anyone else. It means that all efforts to gain access to intimacy with one will be shared with both, until all parties learn that it is futile to divide. Primacy means that power to decide is in our hands and not the choice of another.

Power. Leaving one's mother and father means that obedience (whatever it used to mean) is no longer an obligation. Loyalty to one's parents meant that their perspective and desire were more valued than those of one's peers or one's own. Marriage ends that loyalty. Of course this doesn't imply that parents can't offer their wisdom or that adult children would be foolish to seek their perspective. The issue is highly nuanced, but when the rubber meets the road, final decisions are incubated in the matrix of the marriage, not outside.

My wife must know that no power exists outside of us that has sovereignty over our lives other than God. I may obey a call to the military, but only if it is my choice to remain a citizen in good standing. My allegiance is not to kith, kin, land, caste, country, company, church, creed, race or social standing. It is to my wife. Any other perspective puts my wife in the role of competing for my loyalty and love.

My spouse must know that there are no other gods in my life but God. And that the prime, if not the soul/sole, means to live out my heart for God is the way I love my spouse. Power of choice resides in the interplay of give-and-take in the marriage. Let me say this with greater emphasis: *marriage is not a relationship in which one person gets their way and the other joyfully complies.* Power in a marriage is a delicate and mysterious interplay of desire, discussion and decision—it is never to be unilateral and authoritarian.

Obviously, many decisions will not be as we desire. My wife and I are about to re-cover three pieces of furniture that we've owned for nearly twenty years. The couches are torn in a few places, and two decorative quilts cover the worn spots. I could live with this situation for another twenty years and then figure we could move to a healthcare facility rather than purchase new furniture. My wife has been patient and, according to some of our friends, saintly to the point of sainthood, but she reached her breaking point when a guest stood over one couch and stared. I was finally shamed into the expensive process of having new covers put on the furniture.

To be honest, I'd rather buy a sailboat and move our most prized possessions to a sleek, comfortable thirty-seven-foot Halley-Rassy sloop. It isn't going to happen, but we struggle to accommodate our divergent and often contradictory desires. She gets the couches re-covered, and I get a subscription to three sailing magazines.

No matter how difficult the choice, the decision is ours. If this is true with regard to parents and families, then it is equally true with regard to our past.

WALKING AWAY FROM OUR PAST

To leave our parents means we are creating a new world, a new culture. It doesn't mean we lock-stock-and-barrel toss out all we were or all that we've enjoyed from the past. Even if we wanted to do so, we can't wholesale be free or flee from our history. We are embedded in our world, and any extrication requires immense time and commitment. It is not like dropping one's accent and affecting a new way of being. Such changes are at best superficial and self-defeating. We can leave our past only to the degree that we've made peace with it.

The issue is again loyalty. Am I more loyal to my class than to my spouse? Am I more loyal to my fraternity, school, profession, friends, region, hobbies or car than to my spouse? Loyalty to a team, for example, is not hard to discern. The rabid sports fan who dresses in the colors of his team, writhes in their defeat, rises in their victories, and knows more about the details of the players' lives and stats than he knows about his wife and children is an easy mark to condemn. The same is true to a lesser degree for any tangible false god. But what is most difficult to discern is *loyalty to a way of being that comes from a wounded past.*

No one escapes harm. And we all learn to adapt, manage and function in our own way. We learn to tell jokes or avoid offering our opinion. Or we become easily defensive or accommodating. We withdraw or explode. We each have learned to keep pain at bay and pleasure at a premium, and those ways of being are neither fully good nor bad, nor are they neutral. They are a complex fusion of our dignity and depravity and require us to ponder the question: *Who might I be if God were fully and completely to rule my heart? Who might my spouse be if God were fully to seize and own their heart? How would we each be different? What might we be like if our marriage were fully invested in the gospel?*

Recall the meaning of marriage:

> Marriage is meant to be a space where the most holy and intimate
> God shows himself as compelling and good. It is meant to work—
> not easy, not always and not without his presence. Nonetheless,
> marriage is meant to be a relationship that shouts to the world: "He
> is glorious and good!"

Marriage is meant to transform each partner and through the merger, the interplay of two new beings, reveal our great and gracious and most surprising God. Any other purpose for marriage is too small. Any other purpose will fail to enlarge the heart. But this requires that a couple leave the past by naming it, embracing the good and dreaming of redemption.

Naming the past. It may seem simple, but naming our past takes a lifetime. It is the most central and revolutionary part of the process of personal transformation. We can never change what we fail or refuse to name. Leaving our past involves naming what has marked us for ill; embracing our past names what has been used to shape us for good. Sometimes the same event has brought both good and ill.

A friend described the experience of her parents' divorce when she was ten years old:

> I was only on this earth for ten years before my life came nearly to an end. When my Dad who was my hero and my shining star left I thought I'd never be able to breathe again. It shouldn't come as a surprise that that summer I had my first bout with asthma. I learned to hold my breath with the hope he'd come back home. I became a dreamy girl who didn't want to have much to do with reality. I still struggle with staying connected to my husband when he is angry or when I fear he may leave. But I've also seen how much my imagination grew to believe that another world overlaps what is seen. My writing and my creativity came to exist because the pain compelled me to see into other realms. I'd trade my imagination for having a father, but on the other hand, my pain introduced me to a Father who I believe inhabits not only my imagination, but heaven.

I love listening to her prose and poetry, but I'm sad for what it cost to birth her gifts and passion. Naming calls us to enter realms we might have chosen to avoid for a lifetime.

Embracing the good. My friend has named her flight from reality when things get tense with her husband. Dealing with her past has required her to name far more than flight. She is apt to get busy, procrastinate and then find fault with anything she accomplishes. She has many patterns that have bolstered her tendency to flee from the empty space her father left.

Leaving the past is not a choice to get over it. Life is not that easy. It is not a choice, it is a life direction. The direction required to leave the past involves embracing how God has written your past to make known his goodness. Whether we are wrestling with tragedies like past abuse or struggling with our body image and the size of our nose, we must begin with the conviction that God has written our past, our body and our story for his glory. Yet to embrace the past is not a sweeping, global act of praise. It is not a pious "Praise God anyway." Such nonsense really is a flight from the hard labor of entering our heartache to see the markings of God.

Embracing our past is simply holding on to the glory God has woven in us even when we don't comprehend or appreciate what he wrote for us to experience. It is a refusal to deny his presence in spite of our confusion or fury with him. A marriage is the prime stage for applauding and glorying in the performance of God's goodness.

My wife melds hilarious wit with the kindest heart I've ever known. Seldom a day goes by that I don't shake my head or laugh uproariously at her mostly unwitting wit. It was born from the tensions and struggles in her childhood home. Her way of handling pain was to make her father laugh. My wife doesn't believe me, but she is a stand-up comedian.

To leave our pasts together means we must know each other's story and the gold that has been woven through the cloth of our suffering. But it is not enough to prize what is lovely from the past; we must join together in anticipating the promise of redemption.

DREAMING REDEMPTION

Leaving together aims at a conjoint journey to redemption. Leaving is not merely meant to help us grow in trust for each other. If that were the only goal, it would be too small. Leaving is intended to put us on a path that takes us from comfort and control to the uncertainty of God's calling. We leave our parents so we can grow in trust of God. We leave to follow the dream of meeting God.

And it is in the space between us that God intends to show himself. In the middle of a mean-spirited, embittered, unholy tête-à-tête he intends to shine redemption. After I turn my back on my wife, God intends to shake the bed with desire for reconciliation when I'm aware only that I want her to disappear. He prowls the dark moments to seize the unsuspecting heart with dreams of redemption. And we cannot dream, nor travel to the redemption he dreams for us, until we come to speak God to each other.

The call to leave soon requires a married couple to weave their lives together. To weave is to merge soul and heart through the spoken word.

SIX

Weaving

Connecting Communication

This explains why a man leaves his father and mother and *is joined to his wife,* and the two are united into one.

Now the man and his wife were both naked, but they felt no shame.

GENESIS 2:24-25

A marriage is only as good as a couple's ability to fight. A husband and wife who fail to fight are not alive or honest. Every now and then an older man or woman tells me they have been married for fifty or more years and have never spoken a cross word or had an unpleasant discussion. I don't believe a word they've said, though I don't doubt their sincerity.

Somewhere in the marriage a decision was made to be pleasant and avoid conflict at all costs. It isn't that unpleasant conversations or cross words didn't occur; they simply remained subvocal, hidden under the surface. To claim there was never a failure of love—of omission and com-mission—is tantamount to saying they've never sinned. Such a lie is blasphemous.

The fact is we will sin against each other, inevitably. The result of any failure will be hurt and division. It is crucial for us to grapple with the one sure need of every marriage: forgiveness. The process of asking and gifting forgiveness has to do with speech—or how we dialogue when we are hurt. Therefore the command to "weave" or to join together has to do with how we communicate, especially in moments of conflict that will likely require one or both to seek forgiveness.

GOOD TALK

God loves words. His own Son is named Word. He spoke the world into existence through a word. And in due season he will speak Satan out of existence: one single word will fell him. Before Adam and Eve mucked up the world, God used to meet with them at the end of the day to talk. Apparently he enjoyed sitting with them, drinking a fine glass of wine, slicing a hunk of cheese to spread over a piece of thick, chewy bread. He wanted to hear from them firsthand what they had experienced. He already knew, since he is omniscient, but knowing is not the same as being in a conversation.

I believe what I just wrote is true, but if I consider it true, my head spins with the question: *what kind of God is he?*

Apparently he is a God who loves to talk and listen. This is mind bog-gling. If it is true, then it is when I talk and listen that I am most like God. Marriage is supposed to be a world in which we spend the vast majority of our best time weaving together the threads of our lives through talking and listening. It is crucial to know what it means to talk like God.

Good talk explores reality. The first sentence spoken after Adam and Eve sinned was a question. The question didn't explore motivation or consequences; it simply invited Adam to state the obvious. He was hiding because his sin had opened his eyes to his nakedness. And the question "Where are you, Adam?" was not to ask for information but to expose and explore reality.

Good conversation is open-ended and curious. It is not a debate, nor is it mere information giving. There are times for a strong presentation of one's views or to dispense of information to make a decision, but ultimately these are only to serve dialogue. Dialogue is a conversation that weaves the strands of one with another. It is intended to create a new pattern.

God's question to Adam was intended to start an open-ended, creative dialogue. It actually brought forth not a conversation but a tirade of blame and contempt. But good talk remains present to the potential that something good may come from our dialogue. It may be painful and exposing; however, if there is sufficient trust, there will be a hope that hard words will take us to a new way of seeing and being together.

In some ways good talk is like brainstorming. There must be freedom to think outside the box and to explore what is before us with a heart that can think beyond it. Another way of saying it: We have two ways of seeing reality—close up and far away. We can't perfectly see the foreground and the background at the same time; we must choose one view to see well and allow the other to be somewhat blurred. This means that at all times we lack the vision necessary to see all of reality. To better see what is before us, we need the other to speak in dialogue. Good talk names what is obvious, refuses to hide and is open to new views in order to better see what is true.

Good talk honors differences. This may be painfully obvious: men and women are different. Men and women see the world, speak reality and engage in conversation in ways that are distinctive to gender. For example, social psychologists tell us that the average man will speak approximately twenty-five thousand words a day and the average woman will speak forty thousand. If a woman is a stay-at-home mom with two young kids, then she will use about five thousand words before her husband comes home—mostly by repeating the word *no*. At that point she has thirty-five thousand words left. A man who works in a service industry will likely have said twenty thousand words before he arrives home; by that point he has only five thousand left. No wonder there are tensions around how we talk.

Often the tensions related to gender go far beyond the "amount" issue to concerns about quality. A woman often wants a conversation about relationships and feeling. A man seldom is comfortable in that world. He would rather talk about solutions and process. When my wife is anxious about our son, she wants to think about his character, his inner world, experience and uniqueness. I want to know has he studied and whether she has quizzed him.

Our speech comes from two different realities, and both are important. It is simply an issue of which is *more* important. Most of the time an individual believes his or her perspective is "truer" and therefore more important. And when truth claims vie for primacy, seldom is there true, open-ended, curious dialogue. The style has changed to monologue with blame, accusation and/or contempt.

The great killer of all conversational intimacy is contempt. Studies done by John Gottman at the University of Washington's "love lab" have found that contempt is the best predictor of whether a marriage will make it or end in divorce. The greater the presence of contempt, the higher the probability that a divorce will occur.

Honor esteems the other rather than tearing him or her down. A conversation with honor presumes that the other has something to say that is different, and that differences are good, not bad or dangerous. The different will stretch and humble us; it will call us to put aside our presumptions and receive the reality of the other.

Good talk pursues intimate truth. The goal of conversation is the Trinity. God is three and one. He is diverse and unified. The Father, Son and Holy Spirit are distinct and serve each other with joy and passion. They love the pleasure of bringing each other joy. The goal of a conversation about who will take out the trash, where we will vacation this summer, who will win the Super Bowl, whether my outfit looks good, how we will spend the tax refund, and whether we will make love or go antiquing has to do with a love of intimate truth.

Truth is troth, or trust. Truth is a commitment to see reality as God sees it. I can't. I don't. But I may make progress toward seeing reality if I hear my spouse and allow her sense of reality to collide with mine. On each topic I mentioned in the previous paragraph, my wife and I have differed. The only one in which the difference didn't matter was who would win the Super Bowl.

Let me pick one of the others: where to go on summer vacation. She wants to go home to visit our parents with our kids; I want to go away without the kids and far from any home. She wants to connect with our family; I want to be alone with my wife. Both are utterly good and true, and both can't happen the same summer unless we compromise and cut three or four days off each plan.

It was easy at first for her to accuse me of being selfish, and I attacked her for being idealistic. And this brings us to the topic of bad talk.

Bad Talk

Bad talk hides. Bad talk often never occurs in a marriage because the couple refuses to explore reality. They know what will offend or incite the other and simply choose not to walk into that DMZ. Most marriages have well-demarcated DMZs. I know that when my wife brings up her parents or in-laws, sparks are going to fly. And so we avoid it, or if it must come up, we dress for the conversation in fighting attire. Before the first words are spoken, our heart rate is elevated, our bodies' chemicals of fight or flight are simmering, and the chance of productive conversation is nil.

Bad talk first fails to name its bias and its motive to win. We hide either what we feel or what we want. And when we hide, it is inevitable there will be blame and distortion.

In the conversation about summer plans, I failed to admit how lonely I felt and how distant I feared we were becoming because of my work travel schedule. I didn't want to bring it up because I wanted the vacation to cure the travel issues; that would be easier than addressing the exhaustion of my work schedule.

When the issue of why I was traveling so much came up, I defended myself against my wife's words by blaming her for some of our financial struggles. Hiding often shifts to blaming.

Bad talk blames. Bad talk attacks, blames and dismisses the other with contempt. Contempt is a belittling of the other, of their words or motives. All effort to make the other person small is an attempt to make yourself big, powerful and in control. Any time you huff and puff and try to blow the other down, you are operating in contempt. Contempt shows itself in the tone, the eyes and the content of a conversation. Whenever it shows up, true talk is done. It is pointless and in fact harmful to proceed once the cancer of contempt shows itself. It must be named and transformed before the content of the conversation has any hope of becoming intimate truth.

Contempt is the modus operandi of evil. In fact, the name Satan means "accuser." Accusations are generally not invitations or explorations; instead they are assaults intended to humiliate and disempower. ? goal of contempt is to discredit and steal dignity so the victor can 'n in control, unfazed by any different view of reality that is offered.
ir argument over the summer vacation, I accused my wife of be-
'y, controlled by her family and insensitive to my exhaustion.
l me of being selfish, insensitive and lazy. The problem with
'ons is not that they lack truth but that they are not stated
or each other through a pursuit of the truth. An accusa-

tion is (partial) truth used to distort a larger truth. All contempt ends up obscuring the real issues.

Bad talk distorts. Bad talk is like having sand in one's eyes. It blinds. But it is far worse than sight's being temporarily distorted. Our natural tear and blink responses work to correct the problem of having sand in our eyes. Such a natural cleansing mechanism does not exist for speech. The Bible is clear that our words are like a spark that can inflame and destroy a forest. We can easily mar a relationship with an untoward word. And the result is seldom a natural self-cleansing; instead we usually distort the problem further by defending or withdrawing.

A defense is usually either an effort to explain what we meant and thus take away the hurt or a commitment to present ourselves as innocent and blameless. Hiding serves only to keep the ill feeling from being seen in order to keep peace, but then it ferments and becomes a bitterer brew. Whatever the original hurt, it will be exponentially worse. Sadly, what then often occurs in a marriage is cowardly compromise.

Compromise can be a glorious way to weave a new pattern from different strands. The new pattern may hold a beauty that one set of threads could never have created. This is good. But when a compromise is merely an effort to avoid conflict or the hard work of naming contempt, then it is destined to divide, not unite, even when the result initially seems to be peace.

My wife and I struggled with the hurt of our accusations and the distance caused by contempt. First we divided, and later we both came back to the table willing to do what the other wanted. At first that seemed good. It wasn't. We were looking for a quick cure that would rush our marriage to health rather than entering the smoldering ground of our failure.

It is not enough to resolve a problem or even communicate bette' these elements must be woven together with a third kind of strand: t blood-red strands of forgiveness.

REDEEMING TALK

There are three strands that are to be woven into our dialogue: yours, mine and God's. The mystery of intimacy is not that it occurs between a man and a woman but that a third party is privileged to be included in the most intimate exchange of words and eventually bodies. As we talk, God is ultimately the means by which we converse and the end to which our conversation is meant to move.

Let me quickly clarify: a conversation doesn't have to be about God to be about God. It is of course not wrong to theologize together. Many of the most intimate conversations I've had with my wife have involved imagining God together. And theologizing and imagining can occur in prayer, a casual conversation or a fight.

Redeeming talk, however, acknowledges that God is an intimate player in our moment. My wife's and my involvement as speakers for Family Life has taught us to say in tough moments, "I am not your enemy." The number of times that phrase has saved us is legion. It is a time-honored and well-rehearsed sentence that transports us from the debauchery of our sin to another realm in the blink of an eye. This is different from the magic of abracadabra, for it reminds us of why we are not enemies: we have a common, undying, relentless, wild third presence in our marriage—God. He is my friend and he is my wife's friend; therefore whether we like it or not, he intends for us to be friends and not enemies.

Redeeming talk borrows hope from God to risk another encounter. In ', not just one encounter but seventy times seven. This is the most ndish component of marriage—the willingness to reenter a marred with hope.

these words must be weighed carefully for their intended laving a heart to forgive seventy times seven does not mean ndly walking back into a dangerous or demeaning situation abused in the same fashion. When a woman reenters an sically or sexually abusive situation after her husband has said, "I am sorry, please forgive me," it must be because his words are grounded in a willingness truly to repent, not merely to voice sorrow. Words are like paper currency. If a bill is not backed up by gold, then it is a mere symbol without substance. When emotional, physical or sexual harm has been done, the gold behind the words must be a willingness to seek help and accountability that would bring real and significant consequences for ongoing failure.

Redeeming talk confesses God's presence, my failure, your hurt and our desire for the mystery of intimate truth to bring us to a new union. It begins with one of the most radical premises of the Bible: all problems in my life are first and foremost my own and not yours. Jesus tells us: "Do not judge others, and you will not be judged. For you will be treated as you treat others. The standard you use in judging is the standard by which you will be judged. And why worry about a speck in your friend's eye when you have a log in your own?" (Matthew 7:1-3). If this passage were believed and lived, it would end the vast majority of bad talk. It might not carry us to redeeming talk, but it would at least cut down the chronic presence of contempt.

Redeeming talk owns our failure and then asks for favor, for grace. It owns the status of being undeserving, needy and broken. To ask for forgiveness must go infinitely beyond saying the words "I am sorry, forgive me." It must enter the pain of the harm. It must walk through the brokenness of the other without hiding, blaming or distorting. And it must comprehend what only the eyes of God can provide: a perspective on the harm that doesn't lose hope.

If we enter the harm with hope, not of merely rectifying or getting over the hurt but anticipating the healing balm of God's forgiveness, then it is possible to dialogue about the failure of the process and reenter the subject matter of the conflict without having to create another DMZ. The result will be growth in humility, play and passion.

S E V E N

Weaving

Bringing Our Souls Together

Good talk leads to soul weaving. The weaving together of two souls is the creation of a piece of art that is more costly and beautiful than any Rembrandt, Monet or Chagall. It is the most beautiful of all God's creation; it is delicate and rare. It is to be strived for, and we need to acknowledge that it doesn't come easy or often, even to a good marriage. The fact that it is rare ought not to be discouraging; instead its rarity is meant to invigorate our search for this pearl of great price.

Perhaps it is like any highly evolved skill. It takes time, patience and a passion to pursue to near perfection. Few wish to take the time to achieve such skill when getting by with a C is sufficient for most and a B seems more than enough. Many couples will be satisfied getting along, staying relatively conflict free and enjoying each other's company. Communion need not go any deeper.

It is relatively easy to help a couple satisfied with a C or a low B to achieve their goals. In fact, we can give you five steps to achieve comfortable mediocrity.

1. Listen longer than seems reasonable, and always be four times more positive than critical. This is a wise thing to do. However, it implies the necessity to avoid conflict. It assumes that marriages fail if they are embroiled in fighting or if they don't avoid conflict. But actually there are times that listening must move us to jump into the raging river of conflict rather than sidestep it.

2. Be slow to express anger. Count to ten before saying anything when you are irritated. This too is a good thing. But it implies that anger is a problem and should not show up in marriage. Anger *can* be destructive, but its absence is actually a sign of unhealthy people or a fragile relationship.

3. Never question another person's motives or suggest that what they are saying is not what they mean. It is wise not to repetitively tell a person that what they are saying is not what they mean. Worse, it is debilitating to be with someone who is constantly telling you that your motives are wrong or that you are not telling the truth. However, the only way we can know our heart is in dialogue with someone who is willing to press beyond our logic and protestations of innocence.

4. Avoid conflict by choosing to do what the other wishes whenever possible. It is wise to avoid silly conflict. Pointless disruptions can be escaped if we simply do what the other person wants to do. However, a pattern of compliance will always lead to resentment and passive-aggressive sabotage. It is crucial to wisely encounter our differences and to do so with both conviction and openness.

5. Work constantly to lower your expectations of what a marriage might be. This seems extremely reasonable, but it is the death knell of passion. We learn quickly that what we want will not easily, if ever, come to fruition. But to kill desire by erasing dreams is to orient the heart merely to survival. It is not honoring to relationship or the promise of the coming God.

The first four suggestions reflect some wisdom; the final principle is immoral. There are many other principles that might enhance the quality of life and communication, but these four will virtually guarantee a C-to-B level of intimacy. The rub is that these principles bespeak efforts to "get along" and are not designed to help a couple grow personally or as an intimate union. A good question to ask is, is mediocrity immoral? If your answer is no, then all five principles will work. But there is much more to be enjoyed if we are willing to give up the status quo and press on to the high mark of maturity in love.

Soul weaving requires time, story, dreams and risk. Let's explore what is required in each dimension.

TIME

If you are satisfied with a C marriage, get together with your spouse at least once a month. If you want to raise it to a B, then have a date night once a week; of course that won't happen, so making it two out of four earns a B-, and three out of four will give you a solid B. If you want to go higher, it will require not much more time but a world more intentionality.

For most people time is a more precious commodity than money. Time is a priceless gift that states with great clarity, "You matter." Many couples simply don't take time to talk. They allow touching base during the fifteen-minute drive to the gym or a hurried conversation while getting a meal on the table to suffice for conversation. The proper response to this is "You're crazy." Especially if you are sitting in front of the television or in separate rooms, carrying out life at a distance of ten to fifteen yards.

Time requires two key commitments: exclusion and reflection. To say yes to time together I must say no to all else. Life has a way of interrupting and erupting just at the point where we have planned time for ourselves as a couple. That is evil's plan to keep us from growing together. One must be fierce and relentless to carve out the time, protect it and then use it when it comes. It is much easier to plop into bed or douse oneself in inertia in front of the television than to put coats on and go out the door.

Without reservation we recommend: Get out of the house. Get away from cell phones, computers, noise, kids, chores and temptations that lurk like minions of hell when you need to be together. Of course your child is not an agent of evil normally. But at the time you've got several hours planned to be together, your sweet bundle of joy can become darkness incarnate. Yes, we are overstating the problem, but if spending time together is so easy, then why doesn't it occur more often?

The real commitment that takes you from a B to an A is what you plan for that time. If you simply go to dinner and a movie, the time is nearly useless. Sitting next to each other at a movie and then driving home may make a nice evening, but it will seldom lead to becoming soul mates. Seat mates yes, a union of heart and soul no.

You must reflect on the time—that is, plan the time—in order for it to be meaningful. We find it helpful to alternate the leadership of couple time. The same person ought not always plan the agenda. Sometimes the agenda of one week follows closely on the heels of what was engaged the week before. But there should be some agenda beyond "Let's go out and talk." If you have no goal, you will be sure to achieve it.

The goal might be as simple as "Let's catch up." Or it could be "I want to read a poem or a passage from Scripture and talk about it." It might be to develop a plan to talk about a topic that has always been volatile and needs to be addressed jointly with a new heart. Or it could be going to a movie and then sitting in a welcoming coffee shop and talking about it for an hour. The particular plan doesn't matter. What matters is that you've put time into thinking about what you want to invite your spouse to encounter and then created a context to make it happen.

STORY

A marriage is a womb of stories. This matrix generates new lives and stories, and in it old stories are brought to a point of completion and redemption. A couple will never become wed in the fullest sense of the word until they become each other's favorite storyteller and listener.

Stories are meant to run the gamut from a glimpse into the day's activities, to mythic tall tales of one's family's origin, to the glories and tragedies of one's personal and corporate past. In our culture a family is inevitably surrounded by stories as the television drones its tiresome fare, DVDs are replayed and music hints at stories embedded in its lyrics. We can't escape stories, nor would we want to, but few married couples make use of their stories for the sake of intertwining their souls.

One of the great tragedies of a divorce is the loss of stories. If you divorce, to whom will you tell the stories of how you met, the birth of your first child, the day the phone call informed you of your father's death? It is not merely the future that is lost in divorce; it is also the past. The tearing apart of stories is one of the heartbreaking losses that can never be mended. How much more obvious can it be that the telling and honoring of stories is meant to be a rich part of a marriage?

We honor stories together when they are not only told and heard but entered to experience more than has been said. A good rule of thumb: every story once told opens the heart to new data in a new telling. But that won't occur unless the listening spouse is curious and reencounters the story with the sensitivity of a fresh hearing.

I had heard the story of my wife's decision to attend Colorado State, but it wasn't until I heard her tell a friend about the decision that I actually heard how hard it was for her parents to let her go. I must have known the data, because I was not surprised, but I had never asked her how her folks tried to talk her out of going and what had led them to eventually give their blessing.

As I heard further stories from that period, I was even more amazed at my wife's tenacity and courage. The college decision involved complex family and personal issues, and this choice helped me understand the meaning of other events that transpired during that season in her life.

Story helps us interpret story, but we will not gain new lenses to see our spouse if we go into neutral when we begin to hear an "old" tale.

Each telling of even the best-known story will contain a word or a phrase that adds a richer perspective than we had before. And each new word gives us the opportunity to enter the other's heart more deeply.

A dear friend told me of a conversation he had with his wife as she told how she had become irritated with a store clerk. Amazed at how riled up she was, he spent a good portion of the first ten minutes saying, "Whoa, now. You are overreacting. It's not that big of a deal." After repeated efforts to tell her story, she just slammed down her water glass, said, "I'm finished," and walked away.

He was about to shrug it off as an odd aberration, but for some reason he followed her to the bedroom and apologized. He said, "I was wrong to try and calm you down. She obviously hurt your feelings, and I don't yet understand why it got to you like it did, but I don't want to end the discussion where we left it."

His wife was stunned. In their eleven years of marriage, he had never before pursued a discussion that had ended poorly. As surprised as she was, he felt awkward but jumped into the deep end. He asked, "What did she trigger in you? Have you felt that way ever before?"

The discussion lasted over an hour. His questions were sincere, and she answered them. The data that came to the surface involved years of feeling patronized by her father and being under constant pressure from her mother not to upset her father. Once when she was a little girl, she said, she had simply asked a clerk for help to try on a dress, and her mother made it a capital offense to have imposed on the clerk. The child had a meltdown and brought that whole section of the department store into a deadly quiet. Her father was mortified, her mother was enraged, and she learned to hate shopping.

My friend was at a loss. He learned a great deal about her father and mother, her hatred of shopping, the fear of making a scene, and her reluctance to ever ask anyone to help. "In about an hour," he told me, "I felt like I was introduced to a woman I knew but had never met." Stories' power lies in opening up a vista of perspective that mere declarative sentences can never provide.

Several months later I talked to my friend's wife about what had happened after that night. She said, "He went shopping with me about a week after I told the story, and he said I had to ask for help. When I got frustrated with myself or the clerk, he soothed me and reminded me that I was on my own and my mom and dad were not there. It may sound crazy, but we've never felt closer in our marriage."

I wasn't surprised. The intertwining of stories past and present brings the deepest sense of closeness we will feel with another human being. If we deprive one another of significant stories, then we also keep our souls from being woven together.

DREAMS

Dreams are stories about the future. If we have the courage to enter the past, then it is our calling to let the past speak about the future. Dreams don't just spring up inside of us without a context. Desire is always attached to stories.

My wife and I knew that we would have additional dollars to spend at the beginning of the year. I knew she wanted some new "house stuff," but I couldn't see a thing that needed to be changed. I secretly hoped I could use the money toward the purchase a new motorcycle. I ride daily and make my commute on a bike, and the new model of my current bike had better brakes, more power, lower weight and a dozen new engineering additions that made it an imperative purchase.

When we began talking about the money, my wife opened a catalog to show me new sheets, comforters, a duvet and pillows for our bed and for one of our children's. I felt magnanimous because I figured those things wouldn't cost much. When she told me the price, I was speechless.

If you had told me then that to speak and to listen is to be most like God, I would have shot you. If you had reminded me that how I speak either draws us together in a beautiful union or divides us and leaves us vulnerable to harm, I would have agreed but still wanted to shoot you. I saw my new red BMW RT 1150 RTA go up in the flames of old sheets.

The sheets were fine; I slept on them last night. As for my son's room, he wouldn't know he had new sheets on if you forced him to sleep in the plastic they came in. It was all ridiculous, sort of like knowing you must die but then realizing that you are choking to death in a chubby-bunny marshmallow-eating contest. How could I lose my dream, my desire, to sheets?

My desire was attached to the image of mounting a new steed and riding off to work. My wife's dream was attached to the image of a home that is cozy, inviting and beautiful. The most important room for her is the bedroom, and the most important piece of furniture in that room is the bed.

What was required was first to listen, count to ten, and then enter the dreams and desires of my wife and the stories that give those desires meaning.

Dreams shape our future. If I don't know and enter my wife's dreams, then I am dead to her future. What does she want to do, go, be, own, give, learn, teach, love? If I am deaf to her desires, then I will not know her heart nor weave her dreams into our present.

Far more is needed than a discussion that answers the question "What do you want?" That question needs to be asked and addressed on a regular basis, but more important is reading the desire and dreams you already know exist in your spouse and inviting her or him to narrate the stories that give desire meaning.

The dilemma of desire is that most go unfulfilled. Even the ones that do come to fruition, like making the long-awaited trip to Rome, buying a small getaway sailboat or getting a college degree, came with so much waiting and suffering that the journey itself was better than the fulfillment of the dream. Desire gives passion to life, but the meaning of *pas-*

sion is actually "suffering." Dreams aren't fun. They aren't silly or small. They are full of a raw hunger for heaven itself. To enter the dreams of the other without derision, contempt or cynical realism is a huge risk.

RISK

A marriage is a commitment to the other that says, "I will give my heart and soul and body to your protection and provision. I betroth myself to your joy." No one ought to make that pledge without consideration of what it means. However, no one can fathom what it will require to say no to a desired new motorcycle and yes to new sheets.

I know that in the grand scheme of existence the decision to bless my wife's desire, to enter her dreams and the stories surrounding that desire, is a wiser and more honorable course than purchasing the bike. It still hurts. And it bugs me. On the first night of sleeping on the new sheets under the new duvet cover, I wanted to dream about riding my fantasy bike along the undulating curves of a British Columbia forest.

What I was called to do, however, is to ooh and ahh at the gorgeous weave, the softness, the brilliant colors, and then reassure my wife that I am not angry, hurt or even slightly disturbed by our new purchase. And I have done all of the above (reasonably well, even if not perfectly), because I have put in time in prayer and in study of my wife to better comprehend all that this purchase means for her.

The risk of marriage is living by faith and hope in order to live out love for the other. By faith, I believe redemption has come for us. By hope, I believe redemption is soon to arrive for us. And now, if my desire is more about redemption than about anything else, nothing can thwart me but fear itself. If I am willing to risk for redemption, then union is a certainty.

The risk is to open one's heart and then one's mouth. If I open my heart to what I most want for us as a couple, it is neither new sheets nor a new bike; it is the intimate weaving of our hearts in the pleasure of redeeming love. I want my wife to know and to be at rest in Jesus. I know she wants the same for me even more deeply than I want it for myself.

The greatest risk is to believe the psalmist when he says, "Whom have I in heaven but you? /I desire you more than anything on earth" (Psalm 73:25). Marriage is meant to be a communion of souls that arouses our desire for heaven more than any other relationship. And it is to do so paradoxically, through giving us tastes of both our greatest disappointment and our sweetest fulfillment.

No one on this earth has wounded me more deeply than my wife has. No one has ever, or will ever, woo me to the pleasures of heaven more than my wife has and will. That is union. A union of desire that is hard to swallow and hard to fathom, both/and, joined together, wedded, welded, wound together oddly and gloriously. Such a union of souls speaks of what is known through becoming "one flesh."

EIGHT

Cleaving

United into One Flesh

This explains why a man leaves his
father and mother and *is joined to his
wife,* and the two are united into one.

Now the man and his wife were both
naked, but they felt no shame.

GENESIS 2:24-25

🖌

Sex is volatile, and it was meant to be. No other topic bears more potential for intrigue, humor, hurt or hope. It is a loaded issue that can't be
addressed without arousing a variety of strong feelings. Some readers
would rather see this book end on the issue of communication, while
others have skimmed quickly through earlier chapters to get to this one
topic. Sex's volatility is due to the intensity of both desire and shame.

Desire is an ache for completion. Desires for a 1967 Mustang, to work
in an orphanage in Rangoon and to get a graduate degree in counseling

are all reflections of our ache to see the kingdom of God come in its full revelation and glory. We want heaven and every desire is a puzzle piece that when put into place reveals the glory of God's coming. And sexual union, more than any other desire comes closest to the glory that will one day be revealed.

Sex, becoming one flesh, is to marriage what the Lord's Table is to the communion of the worshiping people of God. Mike Mason, in *The Mystery of Marriage*, writes,

> Of all the sensations we can experience with our physical senses, surely this is the one that comes closest to the Lord's Supper in being an actual touching of the source of our being, of our Creator. . . .
>
> Like prayer, sex is a thing of exertion, of sweat and of groaning, and like death it is intimately acquainted with surrender, excretion, and with the mournful frailty and heart-rending glory of flesh. And these are all things that God has made. He made the woman with an open wound in her body, such that it can only be staunched by a man; and the man He made with a tumor, the maddening pressure of which is only alleviated when it is allowed to grow inside the woman's wound. He made the man to root and to flower in the aching earth of a woman. He made sex, we have to suspect, specifically so that it would be difficult for the mind of man to conceive of anything more earthy, more humiliating, or more desirable, and so to be a constant reminder to him of his true nature. But it was also to instruct him in a higher nature, and in his destiny. For in touching a person of the opposite sex in the most secret place of his or her body, with one's own most private part, there is something that reaches beyond touch, that gets behind flesh itself to the place where it connects with spirit, to the place where incarnation happens.

Mason's words are scandalous. By equating sex and spirituality, intercourse and communion, earthiness and transcendence, Mason has disclosed one of the great mysteries of life—the interplay of heaven and earth. Most people would prefer for those worlds to be far more divided, controllable and predictable. It is easy to focus on heaven and ignore, or worse, disdain, sex as too wet, wild and human. Or it is easy to focus on the earth and ignore, or worse, disdain, transcendence as too abstract, mystical and religious.

Sex weds souls and worlds, even without marriage or commitment. Paul warns that even union with a prostitute creates a bond that can't be broken. Sex is not to be entered lightly or without awareness that meaning is created even in casual and random encounters. Sex is volatile, and like a loaded gun, it is to be engaged with respect and wisdom.

The reason for such honoring care is the potential for shame. Sex and shame, in a fallen world, are bound together. It is nearly impossible to be sexual with one's spouse without the bedroom's being filled with a noisy, haranguing crowd. No moment of marriage is meant to be more private, and likely no moment is more invaded by the ghosts of one's past and present. If Paul is correct, then we bear the marks of past sexual liaisons in our marriage. We also bear remnants of shame from past sexual abuse, pornography, perversion and experimentation.

No wonder marital conversations about sexuality tend to be infrequent, strained and full of blame. It is not a topic we handle well; therefore we tend to accept sex as it is, hoping it will improve and quietly finding fantasy substitutes to fill the disappointment and cover the shame that surfaces. No wonder evil finds such ample ground for assault.

The most crucial theological truth about sexuality is that God loves sex and evil hates it. God made us sexual, and he glories in his plan for our union and joy. Evil hates what God loves, and it has found that more harm can be done through sex than perhaps through any other means. Often the chief battleground for the human soul is the terrain of sexuality.

Consequently, sex is not one topic among many, nor is it the most important part of marriage: it is the summation of all that comes before and the furtherance of the process of leaving and cleaving. Here we will consider what God desires for us sexually, what must be done to empty the bedroom of ghosts, and what happens if we choose to remain distant, bored, angry or disappointed.

GOD'S DESIRE

Sex changes when it is seen as a gift from God. As a gift, it is to be honored and cherished as bearing the glory of the One who gave it. Many times even expensive gifts are tucked away in an attic because the gift or the person who gave it is not valued. Yet an inexpensive photograph, if it was given to us by an extraordinary person, like the president of the United States, is framed and set in a prominent place. And if a gift is priceless *and* the giver highly prized, its mere presence brings delight and it is carefully protected. One simply wouldn't toss around a Stradivarius or let a neighbor's son take it to show and tell.

Sex is God's Stradivarius for a couple, and he intends for the gift to be well cared for and used. But first he requires us to leave and weave. In leaving a new couple establishes a foundation of trust—a confidence that we are more important to each other than anyone or anything else. Sexual intimacy is built on the promise of exclusivity. There is no one else I desire, nor anyone who will take me from you. A partner who is uncertain about their spouse's loyalty will never be able fully to surrender their heart or body to the other. The result will be fear or suspicion. It is impossible to surrender to the pleasure of sexual touch if I am tense or fearful. Trust is an utter necessity for sexual joy.

In weaving a couple comes to trust in hope. Leaving enables a strong base of faith to be built; weaving causes a couple to trust that words will be honored, confession and forgiveness will remove the debris of sin, and the future, though uncertain, is sure. Confidence in the future grows because the promise of the spoken word is found to have substance.

A promise may be quite small, like the promise that I will be home by 7:00 p.m. If I am late, I will call beforehand; further, tardiness and excuse making will not become a pattern that you are forced to endure. My words are true and trustworthy.

Over time, arguments will expose our failures, yet we will be even more solidified because we have the ability to name our sin and ask for forgiveness. Some patterns may be struggled with repeatedly, but our hope is not so much to completely eradicate the sinful as to be able to address it with honesty and tenderness. The more we see our words transform each other, the greater our confidence regarding the future will grow.

The gift of hope produces a greater willingness to risk. Sexual joy requires risk to grow, but without the safety net of promises kept, few will risk being playful and free. Sex often becomes dull and predictable because the couple has failed to kindle romance. The problem may be resolved by a night away and a few good suggestions to help rekindle the flame. But when the sludge of years is not washed away by a change in venue and plan, this is likely due to a failure to grow hope through weaving.

A couple must have a good feeling about the past and the future in order to be present in the here and now. Consider the psychological debris of an unresolved past and an unsure future. An unresolved past brings regret, which causes us to ruminate and to be filled with guilt. An unsure future leads to worry and hypervigilance. The result of regret and worry is distance or dissociation from the present. Bonds of marriage are strong only to the degree we can join together without the weight of regret or the mania of worry. Only faith and hope provide an antidote to those diseases. Faith will not grow without a couple's leaving; hope will not develop without their weaving.

The failure of most marital sexuality is found in a couple's failure to leave and weave. Sex is a powerful elixir that can numb the awareness of other marital tensions, but over time it will lose its ability to connect and cover over unacknowledged struggles.

God designed sexuality to be the context where love is experienced in a wash of sensual pleasure. Faith and hope are both in service of love. Love can be defined as the giving and receiving of pleasure for the glory of God. It is not mere give-and-take but giving that brings the other pleasure—thus a receiving of their joy due to our sacrifice. Sex is meant to be self-satisfying sacrifice—giving to the other just as much in receiving pleasure as in giving it. As I please my wife, her pleasure is meant to arouse me; as I am aroused by her pleasure, my pleasure is meant to deepen her joy. The echo of pleasure increases in volume and intensity as it moves to a moment of individual and mutual climax.

Are we speaking about sexual play that moves toward orgasm? Yes; but our words are also meant to describe the joy that all love is meant to bring the other, including the heart of God.

Sexual joy is a picture of God's union with his bride. Sadly, it will not be all he desires for us until we begin to clear out our crowded bedroom.

BEDROOM GHOSTS

If a person says, "We have great sex. We have never struggled in that area," he is not telling the truth. We've met couples who have nothing but sex to keep them together, and it is working. But survival sex doesn't lead to joy; it merely keeps a person intact. It is a form of sexual addiction that is guaranteed in the long run to turn dark.

Every couple struggles, at least in different seasons. Sex will not move to a consummation that is both satisfying and intimate unless both hearts surrender to pleasure—one's own and the other's. Whatever breaks the process of surrender will disrupt the pleasure. The three great killers of pleasure are fear, anger and disgust.

Fear. The source of sexual fear is usually comparison. *Am I good enough, or is there something wrong with me?* This can be caused by an erectile failure or by the inability to have an orgasm or some other sexual dysfunction. The comparison might be made to a specific person ("Am I as good as your first husband or boyfriend?") or it can be in contrast to a whole gender ("Am I attractive to you though my body is not as thin as other women's?"). Every comparison put us either above or below, and when we are below (and there will always be someone ahead of us), there is fear of inadequacy.

The fear is based on the breaking down of exclusivity. If I am not enough, then you will look for someone else. At core it is the deep fear of abandonment and betrayal. It is not enough merely to encourage one's spouse: "You are all I desire. There is no one but you." Like cotton candy, such fluff will suffice for a moment, but the fear doesn't go away unless it is engaged. I must ask my spouse and myself: What is my fear? What is yours? With whom are we competing? What are our body images, and what are the stories that brought us to those beliefs? Am I afraid that your mind/soul/body is more alive to another than to me? Fear can't be ignored, wished or willed away; it must be faced, named and engaged in order for the ghosts of fear to be banished from the bedroom.

Anger. Another host of ghosts are due to unresolved anger. It is impossible truly to surrender in pleasure to someone you resent or toward whom you feel bitter. Your anger may be due to unaddressed hurt that has built up like a pounding headache. The tension of a divided relationship may be bridged at first with sex, but over time the bridge will rot under misuse. It is dangerous to kiss, make up and have sex too many times. Soon one partner, usually the wife, begins to feel that sex is either a game or a detour from the real problem. To feel used is to war with resentment.

A woman generally experiences intimacy through words, a man through touch. There are many exceptions—sometimes a man would rather talk and a woman would rather snuggle or touch. But in either case, usually one spouse finds more passion in touch than in words, and it is easy to make sex either the beginning of intimacy or the finish. The one who makes it the beginning finds it hard to risk with words, and the one who makes it the end often finds it dangerous to begin with touch.

Every couple can find the measure of compromise needed for both to feel safe and desired. It is wise to recall that God's sequential process moves from verbal communication to physical intimacy.

But what happens when there is little compromise or communication? Anger builds up like plaque in arteries. It may not immediately cause heart problems, but over time it will cause a stroke or heart attack. Many marriages end in death or divorce simply because one partner didn't name or the other didn't hear the growing decay caused by unaddressed anger.

It is crazy that many men will change the oil in the car, do routine home maintenance and tend the garden but fail to ask simple questions: "How are we doing?" "Are there any short-term or long-term tensions between us that could become cancerous?" "How do you feel about the way we enter into conflict with each other?" "What would you like to be different about how we fight or don't fight?" A couple can routinely clear out unaddressed anger from the bedroom if they have the courage to name it.

Disgust. The most pernicious ghosts in the bedroom haunt us with shame. Shame is the experience of feeling dark, undesirable and alone. Shame gains power through silence and remains unacknowledged to your spouse and often to yourself, because you feel that disclosure is guaranteed to cause the other to view you with disgust.

Sexual shame can come from past immorality, current sexual struggles or sexual abuse. All three are marked by the experience of ambivalence. Ambivalence is feeling something and its opposite at the same time. For example, I may hate the darkness and self-hatred that come with going on a pornography site on the Internet, but it also feels powerful, arousing and pleasurable. In the case of sexual abuse, a child or adolescent may have felt some sexual pleasure during the abuse while also hating the pleasure. Ambivalence leads to feeling divided and crazy. *How could I hate something and enjoy it as well? How could the very thing I despise also give me such pleasure?*

When the ambivalence has no place to be named with kindness or embraced with sorrow, it will go underground and begin to twist into a dark root. What I fear from another—disgust—will become what I primarily feel toward myself. I take on what I fear you feel toward me. For that reason, many sexual abuse victims have experienced not only abuse but periods of promiscuity when they didn't care what others did with their body. Over time, both the abuse and the promiscuity seize the heart with disgust, and the body shuts down. Sex becomes dirty and can be entered into only with numbness. Sex is a duty that is filled with the scent of self-loathing and other-centered contempt. The result will be a sexually empty experience for both husband and wife.

These ghosts can be removed from the bedroom only through honesty, sexual healing and time. It is not a matter of reading a book, attending a seminar, getting a few months of counseling and being set free. Anyone who would offer quick cures or spiritual panaceas not only is biblically irresponsible but replicating the past abuse. But it is not hopeless. Legions of men and women have regained the freedom and the pleasure of God's original intention for their body. Such restoration requires a willingness to enter into sexual danger.

SEXUAL DANGER

One thing ought to be clear by this point: sex is not meant to be easy. We must take huge risks if we are to be redeemed and to know joy in our sexual union. Many couples prefer the tried-and-true missionary method every Tuesday at 9:30 p.m. and again Saturday night, just like clockwork. Over time the kinds of touch or arousal that are uncomfortable are avoided, and the potential for dialogue has been washed away through tears and recriminations. It is better to have some sex than none at all. The majority of marriages are probably in this spot.

On one end of the bell curve are couples who have basically given up and endure a self-indulgent, individually oriented sexual life apart from their spouse. On the high end are a number of couples who know pleasure is of God, love to bring the pleasures of God to their spouse, and do so with initiative, freedom and playfulness.

Whether you are low, middle or high, there is constant danger. For those who are low, there is the danger of acknowledging that sex has become a war zone and must be reentered and fought for the glory of God. For those who are in the middle, the danger lies in naming the incipient boredom that has shadowed their joy. Do you really want more, or will you live satisfied with little? And for those who are high, the risk is just as profound—do you want sexuality to open your heart to the deepest passions of God?

Passion comes from the Latin word that means "sorrow." To truly have passionately joyful sex, we must enter the dangerous heart of God, who knows both profound joy and profound sorrow. It is like any blessing—we are to be grateful for and delight in God's gift, and we are simultaneously to notice how all joy deepens our awareness that we are not yet home.

It is possible to be alone with one's spouse, sans children, lying before a roaring fire on a cold winter night, sipping a fine wine, eating expensive cheese and anticipating the glory of what will transpire, while also being aware that

- many on this planet will never know a moment of such luxury

- this luxury may not be ours to enjoy for long

- this moment doesn't take away the ache in either of us

The fact is that sex is not merely for pleasure; it is an act of defiance. It is a war cry that is meant to pierce the darkness and clamor against evil: "You fool. You dastardly fool. You didn't win!" Sexual joy is an assault against all the powers and principalities that would divide and devour the glory of intimacy.

Cleaving

Playing with Glory

Sexuality wars against evil and enables us to reenter innocence. It is a playful labor of love that reveals the sweet fragrance of God's love for humanity. Sex, like a garden, requires care and tending, but the fruit is luscious and satisfying.

Many couples experience sexuality instead as a war against intimacy that bars the door to innocent play. God intends for a couple to know sexual joy. And as much struggle as it may involve, he doesn't intend for us to suffer shame or despair. He intends through our sexuality to heal us.

Sexual healing begins with desire. Do we want more from each other, from ourselves and from life than we have come to accept as the norm? Or will we hide? The choice is this: we can stand before God naked and exposed, raw with desire, or we can flee, hide and blame. Like any choice, on the front end it seems complex and confusing, but after the choice is made, one wonders what all the indecision and consternation were about. It is the same with regard to sexual healing. Healing comes when we embrace our differences and bless the Creator for his paradoxical plan. It is furthered when the differences humble us and expose our false demands. And it is completed when gratitude and awe allow the heart to embrace the passion of God.

BLESS THE DIFFERENCES

Men and women are different. The simplicity of that observation may hide realities that are far more complex. Men and women are written to reveal God and to make him known in ways that are not quite the same. Men reveal (only to a small degree more) something about God's strength and righteousness. Women reveal (only to a small degree more) something about God's tenderness and mercy. Joined in redemption, they reveal both his strength and mercy; sinfully divided, they expose violence and enmeshment. What is true about the hardwiring of the psyche is also consistent in sexual responsiveness.

A woman is designed sexually to move with poetic leisure—slow, deep and hidden. A man is created by God to move with athletic fleetness—intense, focused and unambiguous. Women percolate and men boil. Through the interplay they season each other so that grace becomes fierce and strength kind.

There are four stages of sexual movement, and each reveals a fundamental difference between men and women:

- Desire: Sexual focus, interest and arousal begins
- Plateau: Arousal intensifies desire, and vasco-constriction progresses to the point of penile and clitoral erection
- Orgasm: Climax of pleasure
- Decline: Arousal decreases and tumescence ends, accompanied with greater rest

Consider God's design:

	Men	Women
Desire	sight oriented	relationship oriented
	rapid/seconds	slow/hours/days
Plateau	rapid rise	slow progress
	intense/focused	undulating/fragile

Orgasm	singular	multiple
	expulsive	reverberation
Decline	rapid	progressive/slow
	desire sleep/distance	desire touch/talk

God has designed a man to be the mirror opposite of a woman. His arousal is quick and his rise rapid, and he is susceptible to an abrupt and premature ejaculation. His capacity for an orgasm at the point of climax is singular. And the final stage of decline crashes like a plane falling out of the sky.

A woman is the mirror opposite of a man. Her arousal is slow, and the rise to plateau is fragile and easily disrupted. Theoretically she can experience more than one orgasm, and after climax there is often a desire to cuddle, talk and glow in the embers of the moment. One must say the Designer intended such competing, contradictory and complex differences.

What is God's intention? It is quite simple: sex can't be fully enjoyed without sacrifice and surrender. Sacrifice calls each of us to give up something that is legitimately ours—our body. Surrender requires me to turn over what I give up to another's pleasure.

We sacrifice when we give ourselves to another. When we are sexual with our spouse, we give up the comfort of remaining clothed and safe. To enter the realm of another person's desire for the sake of bringing them joy requires that we give up control.

We surrender to pleasure simultaneously, my own and my spouse's. If it were only one, it wouldn't be as complex or as rich. This is not a sequential process—I please you and then you pleasure me. It is in service that we are served; it is in giving that we are gifted. And as we experience skin-on-skin cyclical pleasure, the echo of gratitude and praise grows to a crescendo that allows us to rest in God's arms, momentarily amazed and satisfied.

True sexual joy can't happen if there is resentment or contempt of our differences. If the man complains about the woman's slower percolation, then fear, anger and disgust will grow in both husband and wife. If a woman shakes her head in irritation or disgust that her husband can be aroused so quickly through sight or mere intimation, then she in turn despises the way God has designed the man.

We must bless the difference. Not only is it God's plan, but sexuality stretches and humbles us, requiring that we simultaneously bless how we have been made and glory in the radical demand placed on us by the other—the being who is us and utterly unlike us.

To be faced with strange and contrasting otherness calls us to enter the mystery of God's immanence and transcendence. He is with us—he is like us. He is utterly apart from us—he couldn't be any more different from us. How can we enter this mystery of God's character in a fashion that is at all meaningful? God gives us an analogy through engagement and merger with one who is like us and couldn't be more different. How we bless that human difference will be similar to how we respond to the peculiarity of God. We are to be humbled before God and our spouse; perhaps better said, we are to be humbled before God *through* our spouse. In being humbled, sexual healing moves toward joy.

HUMBLY UNCLOTHED

Healing on any level requires being humbled. James says to us, "Humble yourselves before the Lord, and he will lift you up" (James 4:10). Humility requires us to surrender our self-sufficiency and safety. It calls us to lay down our arms and open our hands to receive. Humility increases desire as we relinquish what at first provided satisfaction.

It may seem difficult to fathom, but we surrender to God through giving ourselves over to sexual pleasure. Sexual surrender is called *sensate focus*. It involves an attunement to sensation, which in turn brings an opportunity to surrender to what is felt, therefore increasing its momentum and intensity. Most people's threshold of pleasure is limited by the ghosts of fear, anger and/or disgust. Or the limits may be due to time, pressure, exhaustion, a barking dog or a phone call that needs to be made in the next hour. Sex, like all worship, is pressured by matters that seem more important. As in prayer, we ejaculate a few words, ask for help, spin a few religious-sounding phrases and close with "amen."

We are not attuned to simple sensual joy. Sexual humility requires slowing down, sensing through smell, taste, touch, sound and sight the orchestrated rhythm of pleasure.

Humility requires that we acknowledge that we want sex to work and be easy, to fill us and not disappoint us. We want untroubled pleasure that requires little and offers heaven and earth. Once I surrender the demand and call it both silly and mad, I can enter sexual union with the acknowledgment of all surrender: "I believe, help my unbelief. I want joy, help dissolve my fear; help my anger; help free me from disgust." A heart of humility enters the bed with naked desire, deep honesty and wistful anticipation.

The result will be both greater pleasure and greater awareness. I will feel more and notice the points at which I no longer allow the pleasure to increase. At that point some questions can surface:

- What keeps me from enjoying a backrub?
- What unnerves me about oral sex?
- Why don't I have the capacity to restrain my orgasm?
- What makes it so difficult to look at my spouse in the face when we make love?
- What is it about this position that seems too unnerving?
- Why can't we share and act out honoring and playful fantasies?
- What keeps me from making love outdoors, or in a car, plane, train, boat?

- Why can't we talk about sex while making love?

Humility doesn't presume that we have arrived, nor does it swagger with the bravado of feigned confidence. A good lover knows there is a world of satisfaction, wonder and sacrifice yet to learn and to experience. Humility is what allows us to keep each sexual encounter fresh and full of romance.

Humility comes to the degree that we are willing to submit ourselves to the glory of the other. Submission in any endeavor, especially sexually, is not equivalent to obedience. We don't submit by simply doing what the other wants us to do. We submit to the other as we bring them a taste of glory. The word *submission* means to align oneself under another person in order to serve a greater good. To submit is to serve the other to help them grow in glory.

A husband who demands oral sex is not to be obeyed—not because his desire is wrong but because he violates love for himself, his spouse and God when he demands anything. He must submit his desire to his wife, and she is called to respond by engaging him. Engagement doesn't mean servicing his desire, complying to his demands or doing her "duty"; instead she is to pursue him. Pursuit might be participating in oral pleasure, or she might say no if she is offended or repulsed or simply doesn't want to do so. Her engagement must not involve contempt for his desire nor fear that he will punish. She is not to harbor anger and use it as a weapon to make him pay for his desire.

Of course engagement must go further. She must plunge into the meaning of his desire, the issues it provokes in her, and a dialogue regarding what it will mean to serve one another so that both know dignity and the joy of desire fulfilled.

Humility calls us to leave our parents, our past and even ourselves in order to be radically faithful to our spouse. It also calls us to dialogue with hope and surrender to pleasure. No wonder sex requires trust and hope.

Growing humility and generosity toward each other soothes the fears, mellows the anger and frees us from contempt toward each other. Shame no longer has a dark and secret place to grow like a cancer and increase its power. In its place are tender shoots of new growth and a promise of fragrant flowers and good fruit. Marriage is meant to be a garden of delight.

PLAYFUL WORSHIP

Sexual healing comes from a joy that is full of awe and gratitude. Sex is awesome. It is bigger than our desire and more complex than the baggage we bring to it from our past. It is big. It is so big that God uses sexual union as one of the prime images of intimacy with him. We are his bride, and he desires to "know" us.

The verb *to know* in the Bible means an understanding of the other that goes beyond the intellectual and involves a physical connection that is found only through sexual intercourse. Such a naked knowing, full of heightened sensual experience, can't be found through any other means. I might learn much about a person through conversation, observation, psychological tests and feedback from others, but such detailed knowledge is not equivalent to the knowledge of sexual union. To be sexually known by another is a revelation of the fullness of our humanity. And it is a window into the God who has designed us to be known through such sensual means.

Sex reveals the heart of God and is one of our prime ways of knowing him and what kind of being he is, what he loves, how he crafts reality, what he desires from us and for us. It is a prime revelation of what it means to be human and to be in relationship with our Creator. Our awe of sex ought to cause us to be wide-eyed and amazed that God would tell us so much about his being through an act that evil has worked so hard to mar and mock.

We're to be in awe that God so deeply loves beauty, arousal, touch and consummation. We see this particularly as God laments the loss of his intimacy with his whorish wife Israel. In Ezekiel 16, a passage rich with sexual themes, God saves a baby girl from death. He takes an abandoned baby still covered in birth blood, washes and clothes her, and provides for her life. Years later he returns and finds her ready for marriage. He takes her as his bride and makes love to her—he wraps her in his blanket, a metaphor for sexual consummation. The next phrase speaks of cleansing her from the blood that comes as a result of breaking her hymen.

God is profoundly sexual, sensual and tender. There is no embarrassment or reticence in depicting God as a sexual partner with his bride. But over time his bride takes his gifts and her beauty and turns them over to others. God laments:

> Your fame soon spread throughout the world because of your beauty. I dressed you in my splendor and perfected your beauty, says the Sovereign LORD.
>
> But you thought your fame and beauty were your own. So you gave yourself as a prostitute to every man who came along. Your beauty was theirs for the asking. You used the lovely things I gave you to make shrines for idols, where you played the prostitute. Unbelievable! How could such a thing ever happen? (Ezekiel 16:14-16)

We ought to be in awe. God's joy in beauty and his delight in giving gifts to his bride ought to compel us to wonder, *Why is he so enamored with me?* Wonder and confusion with his pursuit of us ought to awaken in me a sense of horror—*how awful that I use my beauty and gifts to whore.* Our awe swings between a sense of the awesome and the awful. What brings us to gratitude is that God entered our world, became flesh, to pursue us in order to be reconciled with his adulterous bride.

Our gratitude will equal the degree to which we are aware of how scandalous it is that God chose to pursue us. We are not owed salvation.

It is gratuitous. His passion to win me is infinitely greater than my reciprocal desire to please him. He is often a spurned lover who bears the heartbreaking disappointment of being spurned in favor of lovers who are vile and degrading. My head shakes in disbelief. *Is what I wrote true? If it is, then how can he bear me, and why would he pursue me?* This is language of awe. But if I rest, even for a blink of an eye, in the wonder of his tender and strong arms, then I am overwhelmed with gratitude that I am not alone, not covered in shame and anticipating judgment. God's love is good news.

God gives us awe and gratitude in order to free us to give to others. The more I know his awesome and awful pursuit of me and the wonder of resting gratefully in his arms, the more I desire to offer those gifts to my spouse.

Marriage is meant to be a playground of grace. It is the context to expose the worst and offer the best, to be exposed as the worst and embraced by grace. And grace makes us downright silly—dancing happy. Grace is a party that swings in the sensuality of good food, drink, music, dancing and stories. Anything less is not merely dull; it is not scandalous enough to meet the scandal of grace with the wildness of worship.

Now we go from preaching to meddling. Most worship services are predictable, staged, repetitive and dull. It's not that good doesn't come of them. God is honored and people are fed and grow. But most worship is neither wild nor scandalous. We simply can't build strong churches in this culture and do things that are outside the norm. And so the bulletin tells us each and every thing we are to say, sing and hear. We follow the book. Sadly, many follow the book sexually as well.

Sexual awe and gratitude are meant to vault us into an encounter with our body and our spouse that is a taste of transcendence—a foretaste of heavenly worship. It is a return to being wild, reckless, free and alive. It is a shout of abandon, a war whoop, and praise for all that is human, earthly, divine and glorious.

Marriage is meant to redeem the desert that has devoured the green shoots of life and turned the ground hard, cold and rocky. It brings the water of life to the arid ground of the soul. And the water is to seep into the parched ground and revive it. Our soul is no different. We are (in comparison to what we were meant to be) a desert waiting to be redeemed, and sex is the wet rain of God that is to bring new fruit and beauty. Once we were a garden, and we will be so again. Let it rain. Let us worship and dance in the rain.

In the Garden

Marriage redeems the desert that has come because of our eviction from Eden. When we were exiled from paradise the earth became a wasteland. The miles and miles of strip malls, billboards and other advertising eyesores are evidence of the earth's groaning for redemption. And not only the earth, but "we believers also groan" as we "wait with eager hope" for our redemption as sons and daughters of God (Romans 8:23). Marriage is our context in which to groan for, wait for and receive the firstfruits of redemption.

The biblical image that is the antonym of Eden is the desert. The desert is a lifeless, waterless, barren terrain full of danger and death. In Israel the desert is not sandy with cactus and long stretches of flat, empty terrain. It is rocky with rolling hills and deeply cut empty riverbeds and canyons that hold the potential for torrential floods. There are tens of thousands of shadowed hiding places under massive rock outcroppings. It is a formidable land.

The desert was a fitting place for Jesus, the second Adam, to go to be found faithful in the face of temptation (Matthew 4:1-11). The first Adam was called to be faithful in paradise; the second was to be found true in what most corresponded on earth to hell. Marriage is as well an entry into the desert, to turn the hard, cold, rocky ground of the soul into a verdant, green, fruitful garden of God.

Many will be offended, of course, by this imagery. As a lovely bride and a handsome groom stand before a well-dressed congregation, after tens of thousand of dollars have been spent to make the day one to remember, no one wants to admit what is true. No matter how mature the bride and groom, they are about to plunge into a desert. They join two separate bodies of sin that will inevitably fail to leave, weave and cleave as God desires. And forgiveness is never enough. Hurt, disappointment, self-protection, blame and division are inevitable. Sin never stops until we see God as he is, and that will only be at death or his return. Marriage intensifies sin. But we know that where sin abounds, grace abounds even more.

The scandal of marriage is that it is doomed to fail, and in its failure we are called to be redeemed. Our culture has come to ignore or despise such paradoxes. There are no cures. There are no four, seven or twelve principles, answers, or helpful hints from Heloise or anyone else. Like sex, marriage is a naked one-on-one, full of uncertainty, trepidation, and the call to faith, hope and love—a glorious risk. For those willing to embark on this unreasonable journey, what waits is the garden of God.

GOD'S GARDEN

Speaking of a garden evokes two common images—flowers and food. A vegetable garden usually contains a number of well-ordered rows of plants that are wholly or partly edible. A flower garden is designed either with order or intentional wildness to flourish with beauty. God's garden is designed to both provide nourishment and prompt worship.

Marriage banishes loneliness and in its place nourishes the heart to grow. Maturity ripens the heart and body to be luscious satisfaction for others. My wife is meant to feed on my body and soul. I am to wash her and give her water for her soul just as Jesus does for the church. I am to do so because my love for her is, for a season, meant to be the closest taste of the good drink and food she will one day enjoy at the banquet of God.

Gardens and feasts are inseparably linked. This truth is obscured in our day. Most of us don't depend on our own garden for our food. Instead we go to a supermarket and buy packages of carrots and bags of grapes. Someone else grew them and sent them to our table. We don't celebrate harvest; we chow our way through the whole year with little regard to seasonal celebration and joy. A harvest celebration, like a wedding feast, is meant to be a celebration of the goodness of God, his provision and the fact that at least today we will not starve. Perhaps, it can be seen as an assault against evil that shouts: "O death, where is your sting?" (1 Corinthians 15:55). Marriage is meant to be a resurrection party that nourishes us to face death and say, "Today I am alive and full."

Marriage also prompts worship. My marriage introduces me to the diverse and wild glory of beauty. My wife came downstairs one day in an older pair of corduroys, a linen shirt and a hand-knit Peruvian sweater I had not seen in years. I couldn't stop looking at her. She straightened up the debris from breakfast, made a few phone calls and turned to catch me in the act of staring. She seemed surprised and slightly embarrassed. My wife of twenty-seven years radiates beauty.

That doesn't change the fact that within an hour we were in a heated and unpleasant dialogue (she would say male monologue) about our son's C in French. But even as we argued I remember thinking how beautiful she becomes when she matches me word for word, tangles with my self-righteous argumentation and laughs at my preposterous demands. I am blessed by the presence of beauty. No one gets to hold her hand like I do. No one can hold her face and stare into her impish, irascible eyes like I can.

My wife has woven beauty into the mantel by which I am sitting. I need only raise my eyes to see a vase with dried flowers and pottery she has created. She has marked me with a love for order, color, patterns, whimsy, Colonial period furniture and Cape Cod style architecture. It was not in my blood before I married her; now it is part of my sensibility.

The garden of a marriage is meant to feed and transform the soul so that it can nourish the heart and reflect the beauty of God. The fact that this can't be done well is what calls us not only to grace but to care. A marriage needs the kind of tending that is consistent with the work of growing fruit and flowers: it needs daily, slow, sacrificial care.

DAILY: FAITHFUL CARE

Early in our marriage my wife and I planted a garden. It took up nearly a quarter of an acre. We had no idea what we were doing. The ground hid the seed for a long season, but a month after planting we saw the first shoots of green. It was thrilling. There was not much to do during those early days other than to watch. But after the plants began to show, so did the weeds. Our young plants seemed fragile, and the weeds were wiry, scrappy bar-room brawlers. We plucked out the weeds to give our tender shoots the opportunity to grow un-fettered by the belligerent brood.

During this season my wife, full of child, had a miscarriage. It was our third, and it broke our hearts. For several weeks we stepped into differ-ent worlds and fled from each other in order to escape our pain. In my flight I utterly forgot that we had a garden. Reawakening two weeks after the miscarriage, I walked down to our garden and was aghast. It was if Stephen King had personally orchestrated the overthrow of our garden by mutant cretin plants. It was vegetative havoc.

I'm not proud of what I did—I fled from the garden and made no ef-fort to reclaim it. Later, in the heat of the summer it looked as if aliens had come to feast on our tender shoots. I felt great shame and have never ventured to plant a garden again in over twenty years. Tending a garden requires a daily commitment to care, or chaos is guaranteed to grow.

Daily care need not require hours, though it may in certain seasons. Daily care involves checking in with each other. It calls us to hear and speak in ways that keep our promise to cherish. It certainly means to pray for each other and together. The Bible tells us not to let the sun go down on our anger (Ephesians 4:26). The sundown challenge is not merely a command to kiss and make up. It is a strong command to see one day, one single day, as the only day that is left. Perhaps you've considered the question "What would you do if this were the last day of your life?" Would you spend it bickering or escaping to a separate part of the house?

The Bible is equally clear: Don't worry about tomorrow, because today has enough weeds to pull (Matthew 6:34). Daily living honors the future by simply doing what needs to be done today. For many couples, a commitment to tend the garden starts with developing a few ritual events that are a part of day-to-day living. Do you have a set-aside time to catch up on the day? After dinner do you sneak away for fifteen minutes to pray? Do you take a daily walk? If you don't have a few daily routines that are solidifying for your marriage, the weeds will win.

SLOW: HOPEFUL CARE

Farmers gamble with the weather, the market and the consumer. An early frost can wipe out a crop. A dump of produce from another country can bottom out the market. Or consumers decide that orange juice has too many carbohydrates, and the value of an orange can drop on mere perception. Farmers live with profound risk, and so does every spouse.

We trust that our spouse will be faithful, will not be hit by a drunk driver and will have some energy tonight to talk and/or make love. Still, most marriages that are faithful lose passion because of the enormous time it takes for fruit to appear.

I went down to the vegetative nightmare a month after I had given up the ghost of care. In a thicket of gnarled and sharp-edged weeds, a random ripe red tomato had appeared. I hate tomatoes, but I was desperate to pluck one piece of fruit for my wife. I wanted proof that our garden could grow good food. I cut myself to bits, but I secured the plump tomato, and I was as proud of it as I was ashamed of my desertion.

It is hard to believe while waiting that a new day will dawn. Yet a marriage requires something other than settling for "reasonable expectations." It requires the unreasonable hope of redemption.

Waiting for redemption is like waiting for ketchup to slide out of the bottle. It takes deliberate, slow intentionality. In the case of marriage, it is the tortoise that wins, not the hare. Hope galvanizes courage, but when expectations are for rapid movement, the result is a burst of change that doesn't carry through the dog days of marriage. Slow wins.

Slow doesn't mean dull and lifeless. The plant makes movement, but it is imperceptible on a day-to-day basis. Over time one can see the blossoms, but it is pointless to measure growth over days, let alone several hours. A conversation with my wife sometimes bursts into fruit months after it was planted. I am so grateful that she doesn't judge me on the one-hundred-yard dash but on a scale that is closer to a marathon's.

Slow requires the confidence that potentiality swarms in the seed. A small acorn has the DNA to one day break into a gigantic oak tree. A movie may bring me to the hard truth that I escaped my father but I never left him. Or a random conversation with my wife may open my eyes to how often I corner her to say what I want. The moments of transformation in my life have seldom come from predictable change agents or in the season my wife might desire; however, change has occurred, and it is mostly through my wife. She has confidence that I will mature; therefore she waits expectantly.

Marriage intensifies our patience as it increases our eagerness. The more we move slowly in anticipation, the more transformation comes, because our marriage has been surrendered to God. Marriage is where we learn to wait for the coming of Jesus.

SACRIFICIAL: LOVING CARE

I watch older men and women more than I ever did before. I suspect it is in anticipation of our day of dying. We can't get enough models to prepare for that departure. What I notice most is the kindness or the cruelty. There seems to be little middle ground in our later years.

The physically stronger one walks more slowly and offers a hand to steady the weaker. When fear or frustration arises, and it comes often, the stronger soothes and gently chides. One can joke about incontinence or spilling soup, but I find such things as comical as a funeral. I don't know God's intention in running out our lives to such indignity, but I suspect it is to give us one final opportunity to be humbled, not so much by bodily failures as by the tenderness of kind care. It may be said that the truest purpose of marriage is merely the opportunity to die for another.

Sacrifice for the other's welfare sometimes calls us to unimaginable acts—such as the first time I cleaned up my wife's vomit after she fell back in bed with the flu. I recalled the phrase "in sickness and in health" from our marriage ceremony, but no one had said, "This means cleaning up the bathroom, gathering the soiled garments and doing the laundry, and then putting a cold compress on her burning forehead." What amazed me about the deed was how small it seemed. She was humbled and appreciative; she treated me like a hero. But it was nothing compared to my desire to take away her suffering. Hundreds of times since then I have experienced the same feeling: *I would do anything to keep my wife, or son, or daughters from suffering, and I can't.*

Sacrifice is not merely cleaning the floor or doing the laundry; it is suffering for, with and against the other without turning away from desire. Sacrifice compels us to enter the heartache, stories, dreams, desires and sin of the other in order to bless them. It calls us to lose ourselves in the complex web of their soul. The mystery is great—in doing so, we find ourselves. We find our truest self and the God who is true to our self. The sacrifices of love open our eyes to the mystery of Jesus' death and resurrection for us.

If marriage reveals God, then it should come as no surprise that the apex of his revelation—the passion of Christ on the cross—must be the heartbeat of all our sacrifice. We are to model him, but even more, we are to be moved by him. Daily the cross I am to take up is the patient hope that soon I may be like him. The more I desire to see him and to be brought to blossoming maturity in him, the greater my gratitude will be for my spouse. Our failures simply serve to deepen desire, call forth courage and plunge us into the war of redemption.

There is but one person's redemption I have signed on to for a lifetime. It is not my child, my best friend, a colleague, a friend or a neighbor. My wife is the only person whom I have covenanted to love until death do us part. My calling is simple: tend the garden I've been given, honoring our season, and with wisdom and perseverance grow her to an astonishing beauty.

And in so doing, delight in the wife (husband) of my youth.

WELCOME TO
INTIMATE MARRIAGE
BIBLE STUDIES

THE GOAL OF MARRIAGE

Why do people get married? The answers may vary, but most would probably say that they have fallen in love and want to be with that person permanently. Or perhaps they would mention their desire for security, partnership, sexual intimacy or children.

This study asks about the *biblical* goal of marriage. The book of Genesis tells us that God created the institution of marriage in the Garden of Eden. It also tells us that he established a pattern for that marriage when he stated that a man leave his parents, weave a relationship with his wife and cleave to her in sexual union. The following six studies look at passages from Genesis as well as elsewhere to explore the significance of these three actions for a good marriage. The last study will point out that the relationship between a husband and a wife is only as strong as their individual and joint relationship with the God who created marriage.

TAKING MARRIAGE SERIOUSLY

Most of us want to have a good marriage. Those who don't have a good relationship yearn for a better one, and those who have a good one want even more intimacy.

We want to know our spouse and be known by them. We want to be loved and to love. In short, we want the type of marriage desired by God from the beginning when he created the institution of marriage and defined it as involving leaving parents, weaving a life of intimacy together and cleaving in sexual bliss.

These studies delve into the wisdom of the Bible in order to learn what it takes to have not just a "good" marriage but one that enjoys the relational richness that God intended for a husband and a wife. This divinely instituted type of marriage is one that will

- Bring a husband and wife closer together
- Understand that marriage is one's primary loyalty to other human beings
- Be characterized by a growing love and knowledge of one another
- Be an arena of spiritual growth
- Allow for the healthy exposure of sin through the offer of forgiveness
- Be a crucible for showing grace
- Reflect God's love for his people
- Enjoy God's gift of sexual intimacy
- Share life's joys and troubles
- Have a part in transforming us from sinners to saints
- Bring out each other's glory as divine image bearers

And so much more! The Bible provides a wealth of insight, and these studies hope to tap its riches and bring them to bear on our marriage relationships.

USING THE STUDIES

These studies can be used in a variety of contexts—individual devotional life, by a couple together or by a small group—or in a combination of these settings. Each study includes the following components.

Open. Several quotes at the beginning give a sense of what married people say about the topic at hand. These are followed by a question that can be used for discussion. If you are using the DVD, you may want to skip this and go straight to the opening clip.

DVD Reflection. For each session we have an opening thought from Dan Allender, at times accompanied by an excerpt from our interviews with married couples, to get you thinking about the topic at hand. This material will provide fresh and engaging openers for a small group as well as interesting discussion points for couples studying together. You will find a question here to discuss after you watch the DVD clip. You can download the DVD segments to accompany these sessions at <www.ivpress.com/ims-extras>.

Study. One or more key Bible texts are included in the guide for convenience. We have chosen the New Living Translation, but you may use any version of Scripture you like. The questions in this section will take you through the key aspects of the passage and help you apply them to your marriage. Sprinkled throughout the study, you will also find commentary to enrich your experience.

For the Couple. Here's an opportunity to make an application and commitment, which is specific to your marriage.

Bonus. These are further ideas for study on your own. Or if you are studying with a group, take time to do the bonus item with your spouse during the week.

We hope that these studies enrich your marriage. We encourage you to be brutally honest with yourself and tactfully honest with your spouse. If you are willing to be honest with yourself and with the Scripture, then God will do great things for your marriage. That is our prayer.

1

KNOWING WHO WE ARE AS HUSBAND AND WIFE

"People are ugly and evil. I just can't trust anyone."

"I believe in the fundamental goodness of my fellow human beings."

▶ OPEN

We hear blanket statements like these all the time. We may even make them ourselves from time to time. In reality, though, people can be annoying or just bland, dangerous, threatening and morally ugly, yet they can occasionally be nice and helpful, and even heroic. How do you view your fellow human beings?

Go further: how do you think of yourself and your spouse?

▶ DVD REFLECTION

What intrigues you about how Dan Allender describes the goal of marriage? What troubles or surprises you?

▶ STUDY

Have you ever reflected on the implications of our origins in the Garden? How might that affect our attitudes and behavior toward other people and particularly toward our spouse? The account of our creation in the first two chapters of Genesis gives us a basis to explore these crucial questions.

Genesis contains stories of beginnings, told not for simply intellectual interest but because a knowledge of our origins is crucial for our self-understanding. In Genesis we go back to our deepest roots, and we come back wiser.

To understand marriage, we need to come to grips first of all with who we are as humans. Who are we, and how do we fit into God's vast creation? In this study we will explore who we are as human beings created by God. In a later study we will explore the significance of the difference in the creation of Adam (male) and Eve (female).

Read Genesis 1:26-31.

26Then God said, "Let us make human beings in our image, to be like ourselves. They will reign over the fish in the sea, the birds in the sky, the livestock, all the wild animals on the earth, and the small animals that scurry along the ground."

27So God created human beings in his own image.
In the image of God he created them;
male and female he created them.

28Then God blessed them and said, "Be fruitful and multiply. Fill the earth and govern it. Reign over the fish in the sea, the birds in the sky, and all the animals that scurry along the ground."

29Then God said, "Look! I have given you every seed-bearing plant throughout the earth and all the fruit trees for your food. 30And I have given every green plant as food for all the wild animals, the birds in the sky, and the small animals that scurry along the ground—everything that has life." And that is what happened.

31Then God looked over all he had made, and he saw that it was very good!

And evening passed and morning came, marking the sixth day.

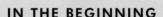

IN THE BEGINNING

The book of Genesis is a book of "beginnings" or "origins." Indeed that is precisely what the name Genesis means when translated from the Greek, and the Hebrew name of the book comes from the first phrase, bereshit, "in the beginning."

Read Genesis 2:7.

⁷Then the LORD God formed the man from the dust of the ground. He breathed the breath of life into the man's nostrils, and the man became a living person.

1. How does God respond to the great array of his creation (1:31)?

2. What is significant about God's creating Adam on the sixth day of creation?

3. God says that humans (both male and female; 1:27) are created in his image. Read the sidebar on what it means that we are created in the image of God. How does this affect how you see yourself?

4. What does being made in God's image mean for the relationship between God and his human creatures?

IMAGE OF GOD

Nothing sounds more uplifting than the statement that we are created in the image of God. Though that's a good thing, what exactly does it mean?

Some people suggest that the image must point to something unique in human beings, since animals are never said to be created in God's image. This would mean that a human trait like reason or the ability to communicate through language marks the image of God in a person.

However, a better route to an answer begins when we ask what an image meant in its Old Testament context. How would an ancient Israelite have heard the word image?

Kings in the ancient Near East would have images or statues of themselves set up all around their kingdom. These statues represented the king and reflected his glory and power. Thus "image of God" in Genesis 1:27 indicates that human beings reflect God's glory and represent his presence on earth. Image-bearers reflect the divine glory. The glory is reflected as the moon reflects the light of the sun. When we look into the face of another human being, we see the face of God.

5. What does it mean that men and women "rule over" the other creatures God has made?

6. In Genesis 2:7 we learn that God created the first person from the dust of the ground and the breath of God. What implication does that have for how humans relate to God and God's other creatures?

7. Your spouse is created in the image of God. How should this biblical truth influence your relationship? (Reflect on both attitude and behavior.)

8. What can make it difficult to see God's image reflected in the life of another person?

▶ FOR THE COUPLE

Reflect on your spouse as created in God's image. How does that perception change your attitude and behavior toward your spouse?

What obstacles keep you from seeing him or her as a divine image-bearer?

▶ BONUS

Psalm 8 reflects on the place of human beings in God's creation. Read this psalm. As you meditate on it, make it specific. Think of the language as describing you and your spouse.

▼

"A LITTLE LOWER THAN . . . "

Some popular versions translate Psalm 8:5 "For you made us only a little lower than heavenly beings." However, the Hebrew clearly supports the New Living Translation (and most other versions), which takes the comparison as between humans and God, not angels.

What does the psalm mean when it says that God made humans (you and your spouse) "only a little lower than God" (v. 5)?

In the same verse, what does it mean to be crowned with glory and honor?

Is your attitude and behavior toward your spouse shaped by viewing him or her as "crowned with glory and honor"? Why or why not?

2

LEAVING—FROM THE MALE PERSPECTIVE

"Your father is always looking over my shoulder. I know he loves you as his little girl, but it makes me feel like a three-year-old!"

"I know your father was handy around the house, but I'm not. Can't we just pay someone to fix it?"

▶ OPEN

How is marriage different from any other relationship you have?

And what impact, if any, should marriage have on previous relationships with, say, friends and parents?

▶ DVD REFLECTION

What are the risks for a man in leaving his parents behind?

▶ STUDY

Read Genesis 2.

So the creation of the heavens and the earth and everything in them was completed. ²On the seventh day, God had finished his work of creation, so he rested from all his work. ³And God blessed the seventh day and declared it holy, because it was the day when he rested from all his work of creation.

⁴This is the account of the creation of the heavens and the earth.

When the LORD God made the earth and the heavens, ⁵neither wild plants nor grains were growing on the earth. The LORD God had not yet sent rain to water the earth, and there were no people to cultivate the soil. ⁶Instead, springs came up from the ground and watered all the land. ⁷Then the LORD God formed the man from the dust of the ground. He breathed the breath of life into the man's nostrils, and the man became a living person.

⁸Then the LORD God planted a garden in Eden in the east, and there he placed the man he had made. ⁹The LORD God made all sorts of trees grow up from the ground—trees that were beautiful and produced delicious fruit. In the middle of the garden he placed the tree of life and the tree of the knowledge of good and evil.

¹⁰A river watered the garden and then flowed out of Eden and divided into four branches. ¹¹The first branch, called the Pishon, flowed around the entire land of Havilah, where gold is found. ¹²The gold of that land is exceptionally pure; aromatic resin and onyx stone are also found there. ¹³The second branch, called Gihon, flowed around the entire land of Cush. ¹⁴The third branch, called the Tigris, flowed east of the land of Asshur. The fourth branch is called the Euphrates.

¹⁵The LORD God placed the man in the Garden of Eden to tend and watch over it. ¹⁶But the LORD God warned him, "You may freely eat the fruit of every tree in the garden—¹⁷except the tree of the knowledge of good and evil. If you eat its fruit, you are sure to die."

¹⁸Then the LORD God said, "It is not good for the man to be alone. I will make a helper who is just right for him." ¹⁹So the LORD God formed from the ground all the wild animals and all the birds of the sky. He brought them to the man to see what he would call them, and the man

chose a name for each one. [20]He gave names to all the livestock, all the birds of the sky, and all the wild animals. But still there was no helper just right for him.

[21]So the LORD God caused the man to fall into a deep sleep. While the man slept, the LORD God took out one of the man's ribs and closed up the opening. [22]Then the LORD God made a woman from the rib, and he brought her to the man.

[23]"At last!" the man exclaimed.

"This one is bone from my bone,
    and flesh from my flesh!
She will be called 'woman,'
    because she was taken from 'man.' "

[24]This explains why a man leaves his father and mother and is joined to his wife, and the two are united into one.

[25]Now the man and his wife were both naked, but they felt no shame.

1. Notice Adam's first task (vv. 19-20). What does it suggest about the role of human beings made in God's image?

2. What lack does God recognize in Adam, in the midst of an abundant creation?

What events or situations in your life have made you aware of your need for others?

WHY POETRY?

Genesis 2:23-25 is the first poem in the Bible. Poetry is the language of song. Adam breaks out into a joyous song when he first encounters his beloved Eve. Later in the Bible we encounter the Song of Songs, a whole book of song-poems celebrating marital love.

3. Why is Adam excited when he encounters the woman?

What does this tell us about the purpose of marriage?

4. What does verse 23 suggest about the nature of the relationship between Adam and Eve, a husband and a wife?

"WOMAN" FROM "MAN"

"She will be called 'woman,' because she was taken from 'man' "
(Gen 2:23). The English wordplay reflects well the Hebrew, where
the word for "woman" (ishsha) is related to the word for "man" (ish).
Again, even the words indicate the intimate connection between the
man and the woman.

5. What does it mean for a man to leave his parents in order to be united to his wife? (Does it necessarily involve a physical separation?)

6. List some of the difficulties that can keep men from truly leaving their parents when they get married.

7. How does leaving parents help a new couple grow closer to each other?

How does not leaving hinder intimacy?

8. What are some other previous attachments, which could hinder intimacy, that are particularly difficult for men to leave?

▶ FOR THE COUPLE

Spend some time reflecting on past commitments that keep you from fully embracing your spouse. Make a list of loyalties from your past that you suspect your spouse would say you are reluctant to break. What would keep you from giving up these past commitments? If you can discuss this without accusation and with a spirit of honesty and prayer, then share your separate lists.

▶ BONUS

Genesis 2 pictures marriage as a remedy for loneliness. Reflect on these questions.

Are single people incomplete?

Are married couples never lonely?

LEAVING—FROM THE FEMALE PERSPECTIVE

"Why do you always want me to cook the chicken your mom's way?"

"Can we stay at home and have our own Christmas celebration this year?"

▶ OPEN

The first step in the establishment of a marriage, "leaving," is the establishment of a new primary loyalty. In Genesis 2:24 a man is called to leave his parents to join in a new relationship with a wife. But the woman must leave as well. What do you think would be some of the particular issues or difficulties for the woman in leaving?

▶ DVD REFLECTION

What are the rewards for a woman in leaving her parents behind?

▶ STUDY

Now we turn to Psalm 45 in order to explore not just the importance of leaving for the couple but also, in particular, for the woman. What does it mean for a woman to leave her parents?

Read Psalm 45:10-15.

^{10}Listen to me, O royal daughter; take to heart what I say.

   Forget your people and your family far away.

^{11}For your royal husband delights in your beauty;

   honor him, for he is your lord.

^{12}The princess of Tyre will shower you with gifts.

   The wealthy will beg your favor.

^{13}The bride, a princess, looks glorious

   in her golden gown.

^{14}In her beautiful robes, she is led to the king,

   accompanied by her bridesmaids.

^{15}What a joyful and enthusiastic procession

   as they enter the king's palace!

1. The princess has come from far away to marry the king. What struggles do you think she had to "forget" her father's house (v. 10)?

2. What do you think the singers mean when they tell her to "forget" her father's house?

3. Do you think the request is fair?

THE BACKGROUND OF PSALM 45

Psalm 45 is unique among the poems in the book of Psalms. It is a royal wedding song, celebrating the union of one of Israel's kings to a woman from Tyre. Many historical questions remain, especially, who is the couple that inspired this uplifting psalm? However, answering such questions is relatively unimportant for the interpretation and application of the psalm today. After all, though inspired by specific historical events, the psalms speak to our own lives. Though we are not royalty, the grandeur of the Psalm 45 wedding tells us something about the importance of the institution of marriage, and a number of the principles expressed in the poem are still relevant. One of the latter has to do with our present subject: the importance of leaving previous commitments as one enters into a new relationship.

4. What do you think it means for the "royal daughter" to honor her husband (v. 11)?

5. How would a wife honor her husband today?

6. Do you think this Scripture teaches that honor goes one way (only wife to a husband)? Explain.

7. Is leaving one's parents in favor of loyalty to your spouse an action you can carry out in a moment of decision and be done with? Why or why not?

▶ FOR THE COUPLE

Talk about any areas of your marriage where you still struggle with issues of leaving.

▶ BONUS

What role do parents have in the leaving process? How can a newly married couple and their parents cooperate in this rather than being at odds?

WEAVING

"I feel secure with her. I trust her."

"He is my rock of Gibraltar. I can count on him."

"We look forward to growing old together."

▶ OPEN

Genesis 2:24 says that a man leaves his parents in order to be joined to his wife. For this to work, we assume that the woman too is to leave her parents and join her husband (see also Psalm 45). Thus in marriage two lives are woven together.

In both ancient Israel and modern society, marriage is a relationship established and governed by law. So this joining involves a legal dimension. A husband can't wake up one morning and decide to have nothing to do with his wife, or vice versa. There would be legal ramifications. But joining involves more than a legal connection. Much, much more than law unites a husband and a wife. What is one thing that has helped you to weave your lives together?

▶ DVD REFLECTION

What does it mean for a married couple to weave their two lives into one?

▶ STUDY

The text we are going to read in Ecclesiastes does not speak specifically of marriage, but it celebrates the benefits of a companion. Marriage is the most intimate type of relationship, and therefore we can learn about marriage from studying what Scripture says about relationships in general.

Read Ecclesiastes 4:7-12.

[7]I observed yet another example of something meaningless under the sun. [8]This is the case of a man who is all alone, without a child or a brother, yet who works hard to gain as much wealth as he can. But then he asks himself, "Who am I working for? Why am I giving up so much pleasure now?" It is all so meaningless and depressing.

[9]Two people are better off than one, for they can help each other succeed. [10]If one person falls, the other can reach out and help. But someone who falls alone is in real trouble. [11]Likewise, two people lying close together can keep each other warm. But how can one be warm alone? [12]A person standing alone can be attacked and defeated, but two can stand back-to-back and conquer. Three are even better, for a triple-braided cord is not easily broken.

1. Reread Genesis 2:23-25 (p. 17), and reflect again on the institution of marriage as established and described here. In what ways do a woman and a man join (weave) their lives together in marriage?

2. According to Ecclesiastes 4:7-12, what advantages are there to enter-

ing into an interdependent relationship with another?

3. While Ecclesiastes 4:7-12 refers to friendship, how do the advantages
   of friendship also apply to a marriage relationship?

THE TRIPLE-BRAIDED CORD

*Ecclesiastes 4:12 speaks of the triple-braided cord: three is even bet-
ter than one. This verse is often misunderstood to refer to the Trinity,
or to a person, their friend and God, although this simple image is
found in at least one other ancient extrabiblical text (Gilgamesh and
the Land of the Living). The argument of the Ecclesiastes passage up
to this point is that having a friend has tremendous advantages—two
is better than one). The concluding verse makes the point that if having one friend is good, having more than one is even better.*

4. What are some concrete steps a married couple can take to weave
   their lives together?

5. What kinds of things can hinder two people from joining their lives together?

How can these obstacles be overcome?

NEGOTIATION AND COMPROMISE

Is it okay to argue and wrangle to convince your spouse of your perspective? Is it honorable to attempt to persuade your spouse of your opinion? Yes, absolutely. Persuasion is a form of rhetoric that attempts to win the heart and action of another by an appeal to emotion, wisdom and vision. What is not honorable is pressure, guilt or coercion.

When you seek to persuade your spouse, it's best to announce your desire to persuade and then launch into a time-limited "presentation" with plenty of opportunity for critique and eventual compromise. The goal must never be to gain your will alone. The true goal of persuasion is the greater good of creating together a plan that includes both perspectives.

6. Does being joined together require that a husband and a wife give up their individuality altogether? Explain your response.

7. How should a couple negotiate their union and their individuality? (Is it appropriate to talk about individual rights in a marriage?)

8. An important part of weaving is how you share your time together. How can a couple tell when a desire to preserve "space" from a spouse is right or wrong?

▶ FOR THE COUPLE

Examine your schedules to see how often you have time together to actually share your lives. What are the obstacles to creating time together?

How can these obstacles be overcome?

Do you have what you both consider to be a healthy balance of shared and individual interests and activities?

Where do you find it easy to weave your lives together, and where is it difficult?

▶ BONUS

Read 1 Corinthians 13:4-8. In light of this text, describe love using your own words. How does the cultivation of this type of love enhance the possibility of weaving two lives into one?

5

CLEAVING

"I don't have words to express the intense, deep pleasure of making love with my husband."

"Our sex life has improved with each year of marriage."

▶ OPEN

Genesis 2, which has established marriage, culminates with the sexual union of a man and a woman. Why would the Bible point to sexual relations as the end point of marriage?

▶ DVD REFLECTION

Why is sex preceded by leaving and weaving?

▶ STUDY

Genesis 2 provides us with a theological foundation for sex in marriage, and thus in this study we return to the second half of that chapter.

Read Genesis 2:18-25.

[18]Then the LORD God said, "It is not good for the man to be alone. I will

make a helper who is just right for him." [19]So the LORD God formed from the ground all the wild animals and all the birds of the sky. He brought them to the man to see what he would call them, and the man chose a name for each one. [20]He gave names to all the livestock, all the birds of the sky, and all the wild animals. But still there was no helper just right for him.

[21]So the LORD God caused the man to fall into a deep sleep. While the man slept, the LORD God took out one of the man's ribs and closed up the opening. [22]Then the LORD God made a woman from the rib, and he brought her to the man.

[23]"At last!" the man exclaimed.

"This one is bone from my bone,
    and flesh from my flesh!
She will be called 'woman,'
    because she was taken from 'man.' "

[24]This explains why a man leaves his father and mother and is joined to his wife, and the two are united into one.

[25]Now the man and his wife were both naked, but they felt no shame.

1. Why do you think God parades all the animals in front of Adam in the quest for a partner suitable for him?

2. What significance do you see in Eve's being created from the very body of Adam?

3. Notice that children are not mentioned in this passage, not even in the statement about the two becoming "one flesh." Explore possible reasons for this.

4. How do Adam and Eve respond to each other's nakedness?

   What permits this response?

5. What is beautiful about marital sexual intercourse?

6. Cleaving follows leaving and weaving. Why is it the third and climactic action in the establishment of marriage? Why is it the end point?

7. Genesis 2:18 cites loneliness as the problem God solves by creating marriage. How does sexual intimacy answer the loneliness problem?

▶ FOR THE COUPLE

In what ways do you and your spouse experience one-flesh intimacy?

What can you do to increase that intimacy?

Describe to each other times when you felt the deepest intimacy with each other.

▶ BONUS

Why is sex such a powerful force in our lives?

THE ULTIMATE
LOYALTY

"There is only one person more important to me than my spouse—God himself."

"Before we became Christians, our marriage did not have a foundation."

▶ OPEN

Fundamental to marriage is the creation of a new primary loyalty. A husband must relate to his wife and a wife to her husband in a unique way. The Bible makes clear, however, that another relationship is even more fundamental than marriage. That relationship, of course, is with God.

What are some ways your relationship with God intersects with your marriage relationship?

▶ DVD REFLECTION

What is the greatest priority of your marriage?

STUDY

Read Psalm 127.

A song for pilgrims ascending to Jerusalem. A psalm of Solomon.

¹Unless the LORD builds a house,
   the work of the builders is wasted.
Unless the LORD protects a city,
   guarding it with sentries will do no good.
²It is useless for you to work so hard
   from early morning until late at night,
anxiously working for food to eat;
   for God gives rest to his loved ones.

³Children are a gift from the LORD;
   they are a reward from him.
⁴Children born to a young man
   are like arrows in a warrior's hands.
⁵How joyful is the man whose quiver is full of them!
   He will not be put to shame when he confronts his accusers
      at the city gates.

A SONG FOR THE ASCENT TO JERUSALEM

A title attached to Psalm 127 (and all the psalms from 120 to 134) is "A Song of Ascent." "To Jerusalem," added in the New Living Translation, is a helpful interpretive addition. These songs were sung by religious pilgrims as they journeyed to Jerusalem from surrounding towns and villages to worship at the temple during one of Israel's great annual religious festivals.

1. How can the Lord "build a house"?

In what ways can you relate to this from your own experience?

2. What does the psalmist mean when he says that it is useless to work very hard?

How does this apply to marriage and family life?

3. What place should God play in a marriage relationship?

4. What particular sin is committed when a husband or a wife makes their spouse more important than God?

5. What, in particular, happens to a wife if her husband puts her first, or to a husband if his wife puts him first?

6. Putting one's spouse first isn't the only way to threaten a strong foundation of marriage. What other things can get in the way and become idols?

7. How does a couple put God first in their relationship?

▶ FOR THE COUPLE

Reflect together on your relationship with God. What do you have to be thankful for?

In what ways can you together deepen your relationship with God?

▶ BONUS

Read Matthew 7:24-29. How does Jesus' teaching here relate to Psalm 127?

How does this teaching relate to marriage?

Then read 2 Corinthians 6:14-18. Does this teaching have anything to do with marriage? If so, how?

What happens if a Christian is already in a committed relationship with an unbeliever?

INTIMATE MARRIAGE
S E R I E S

Other titles in the Intimate Marriage Series
Intimate Mystery Curriculum Kit
Intimate Marriage DVD
Intimate Marriage Leader's Guide

Bible Studies
6 sessions for individuals,
couples or groups in each guide
Communication
Dreams & Demands
Family Ties
Forgiveness
The Goal of Marriage
Male & Female
Sexual Intimacy

BONUS DVD DOWNLOAD

Purchasers of this book are invited to get a free download of the six DVD segments that were created as a companion to the bonus studies in this guide *(The Goal of Marriage)* at <www.ivpress.com/ims-extras>.

Downloads of the DVD segments that accompany the other guides in the series are also available for purchase.